When I go away on a holiday, I like to send a few postcards to friends and family - I enjoy choosing the pictures and the discipline of a very tiny writing space. I love using social media and email too, in the normal run of daily life, but on holiday I have a bit more time to write a card and post it.

And I do like getting cards - I love the clunk of the letter box, and hearing news from friends I perhaps haven't seen for a long time. Some of these cards I will keep - maybe for a few months, maybe for years: it depends on the stories they tell. I can equally well look back over social media conversations and posts, and still have that sense of sharing a life story.

The readings in this quarter remind me of how often God communicates to us through letters and stories in his Word. Paul, for example, conducted so much of his known (to us) ministry by letter - either because of distance or imprisonment; while Matthew's Gospel (our current focus) is full of stories rich with layers of meaning, communicating the good news of Jesus through the centuries.

Every quarter of *Encounter* offers a balanced diet of Scripture readings, and so from the Old Testament we hear about the prophet Amos' passion for justice and the exploits of King David, as well as the aching pain of Job in his agony of physical and spiritual affliction. You can also read in *Worldview* some reflections on praying 'in the desert'- an experience that Jesus shared, and which may be where you feel you are right now.

Sometimes I find, in the bottom of a drawer, a letter I have kept carefully that has encouraged me, challenged me or totally changed my life. Sometimes I get an encouraging email about a sermon I have preached or something I have tried to do (even if not very successfully!). Thank you, Lord, for brothers and sisters down the centuries who have bothered to write words of grace - and thank you for your eternal Word of grace to us in Jesus Christ our Lord.

Sally Nelson
*Editor*

Angela Grigson
*Content Manager*

**ON THE COVER** Claire Dalpra encourages us to explore contemplative prayer without words (pages 75 to 78).
Image credit: Fabio Lamanna/Shutterstock

## THE WRITERS

**MARY EVANS** is a former theological lecturer who still does regular stints as a visiting lecturer at the Ethiopian Graduate School of Theology, and elsewhere. Writing, speaking, church, family, friends and Langham Partnership Board responsibilities fill much of the rest of available time.

**ALISON LO** is a lecturer at Baptist Theological Seminary, Singapore. Previously she taught at the Chinese University of Hong Kong, London School of Theology and Moorlands Midlands Centre.

**MIKE ARCHER** is Vicar of Highfield Church, Southampton. He is married to Sarah and they have two children, Mims and Sam.

**SYLVIA COLLINSON** was a lecturer in New Testament Christian Education and Discipleship in three states of Australia. Now retired and enjoying teaching English at her church to recent immigrants to Australia.

**ANDREW HERON** was a missionary and pastor for almost 25 years in France. He currently serves as Pastoral Ministries Associate at West Church, Bangor, Northern Ireland.

**BRIAN RADCLIFFE** is a recently retired English and drama teacher, and was formerly minister of a Baptist church in the north of England. For the past 20 years he has also enjoyed a parallel career as a freelance writer, specialising in scripts for secondary school assemblies and the use of drama skills as tools for teaching across the curriculum.

**VIVIEN WHITFIELD** is now a self-supporting ordained minister in her local parish church and among deaf people, after many years of Christian service in other directions.

**COR BENNEMA** has a passion to train and motivate people to think biblically, critically and contextually in order to serve in the church and society. He is Senior lecturer in New Testament at Union School of Theology Bridgend.

**CLAIRE DALPRA** works for the Church Army. Her areas of research include fresh expressions for under-5s and their families, fresh expressions for adults with learning difficulties and the sustainability of spare-time led fresh expressions.

## CONTENTS



*Scripture Union, Trinity House, Opal Court, Opal Drive, Fox Milne, Milton Keynes MK15 0DF, UK*
*Email: info@scriptureunion.org.uk Website: www.scriptureunion.org.uk*

*Scripture Union is an international Christian charity working with churches in more than 130 countries. Thank you for purchasing this book. Any profits from this book support SU in England and Wales to bring the good news of Jesus Christ to children, young people and families and to enable them to meet God through the Bible and prayer.*

*Find out more about our work and how you can get involved at:*
*www.scriptureunion.org.uk (England and Wales) www.suscotland.org.uk (Scotland)*
*www.suni.co.uk (Northern Ireland) www.scriptureunion.org (USA) www.su.org.au (Australia)*

## USING THIS GUIDE

*Encounter with God* is designed for thinking Christians who want to interpret and apply the Bible in a way that is relevant to the problems and issues of today's world. It is based on the NIV translation of the Bible, but can easily be used with any other version.

Each set of readings begins with an *Introduction* to the section you are about to study. The *Call to Worship* section at the start of each note should help you consciously to come into God's presence before you read the passage. The main *Explore* section aims to bring out the riches hidden in the text. The *Growing in Faith* section at the end suggests ways of applying the message to daily living.

The *Bible in a Year* readings at the foot of the page are for those who want this additional option.



*Design by Heather Knight*

*Printed by Thomson Press, India*



*ISSN 1350-5130.* 

# JEREMIAH 11–30

## VARYING CIRCUMSTANCES, MIXED FEELINGS – BUT UNCHANGING GOD

In this section of Jeremiah the situation hasn't changed from the first ten chapters. Israel, its people, leaders, priests and prophets had, with a few notable exceptions, shown no signs of repenting for their betrayal of God's covenant or of a desire to turn back to God. Therefore Jeremiah's message to Israel remains the same: God is going to judge you and send you into exile for an extended period. The occasional long-view messages of hope in the distant future begin to creep in, but without a dramatic change in attitudes and behaviour there will be no change in God's current plan for judgement.

However, in the midst of what might be seen as a message of discouragement there is also a lot for us to learn. We see Jeremiah's relationship with God worked out, sometimes with tears and sometimes with thanksgiving. We see who God is and how he works in righteousness and love. We see that God's judgement stems from a profound love for Israel and a desire to see the nation being the people he wanted them to be and having the future that he wanted for them. We see Jeremiah's reflections on previous Scriptures, sometimes explicit and sometimes implicit, and how that influences his own thinking.

I have to confess here that I wrote these notes after a 40-day period when, along with my church, I was focusing on (and trying to learn by heart!) Jesus' prayer for his followers in John 17. That has certainly influenced the way I have read these chapters of Jeremiah and you may notice several implicit connections as well as the explicit ones.

***Mary Evans***

# A CRY FROM THE DEPTHS

**'If we only had this short life, patience would be hard – no time to waste. But for those of us who await eternity, why not be patient?'[1]**

## PSALM 6

I think most of us have times when what this psalmist is feeling exactly represents our own situation and feelings! I am very grateful that for me it doesn't happen very often, although twice in my life I have felt like this for a more extended period and I know that some suffer from this kind of depression and anguish on and off throughout their lives. I am so grateful that psalms like this exist and that there are so many of them. At times when everything feels upside down and desperate it may be helpful for some people to be given lovely verses of praise and encouragement – but I have always found this kind of lament to be most helpful. Not only has someone else felt like I feel, but God has recognised and accepted that feeling and included its expression as part of his own living word. It is OK for believers to feel awful; it is OK for believers to express those feelings; it is OK for believers to complain bitterly about what is happening to them. I like to think that Jeremiah read this psalm and found it helpful when he was struggling with the way his own life was turning out.

However, it is worth noting that this particular lament is not without hope. There is a recognition that things can and will, eventually, change. There is a sense that it is worth praying, because God does hear and does care. There is no indication that the psalmist's circumstances have changed, but his underlying faith in God and his acceptance of the reality of God's love and God's justice remain even if he doesn't actually feel that love at the moment. It is good to remind ourselves that truth and feelings are not always the same thing.

**Take time this week to pray for people you know who are currently experiencing the kind of feelings expressed in this psalm.**

1 Veronica Zundel, twitter, April 3, 2017

 **BIBLE IN A YEAR:** 2 Chronicles 33,34; Psalms 75,76

# 'TERROR ON EVERY SIDE'

**'The LORD is my rock, my fortress and my deliverer; my God is my rock, in whom I take refuge, my shield and the horn of my salvation.'[1]**

**JEREMIAH 20**

In this chapter we see two aspects of Jeremiah's life. In verses 1–6 he is on duty, carrying out the work that God has given him to do, speaking out confidently to Pashur, in spite of just having being jailed for delivering a message that Pashur did not want to hear. In our own generation we have seen power-hungry leaders also seeking to silence opposition by imprisonment and other brutal means. Pashur might have been proud of the nickname Jeremiah gives him, glad to be thought of as bringing terror to his enemies, but his attempt to silence Jeremiah does not change the truth of his original message and the 'Terror on Every Side' (v 3) will be something that Pashur himself experiences rather than causes.

Then, in verses 7–18, we see Jeremiah back at home in his own room, struggling with the opposition that he faces. He has spoken to Pashur about 'Terror on every side', but is very conscious that this is actually his own experience (v 10). He feels let down by God (vs 7,8), persecuted by his own people (vs 9,10) and so depressed that he wished he had never been born (vs 14–18). Like yesterday's psalmist, however, at the same time as he experiences this terrible negativity, he also, underneath it all, understands who God is and what his ultimate purposes are – and finds it possible, in spite of everything, to praise God (vs 11–13). Most of us experience this kind of dual reality at times. We may not be able to copy Lewis Carroll's White Queen in believing six impossible things before breakfast,[2] but we are certainly not always logical in our thinking. Like the psalmist, Jeremiah encourages us to express our feelings, but also to recognise that the underlying truth does not change in the light of our current circumstances or emotions.

**'LORD, my Rock and my Redeemer',[3] help me, particularly when life seems so very difficult, to remember that, when we reach rock bottom, we really do find rock.**

[1] Ps 18:2 [2] *Alice through the Looking Glass* [3] Ps 19:14

**BIBLE IN A YEAR:** 2 Chronicles 35,36; Luke 1:39–80

# SHEPHERDS BAD AND GOOD

**'In your relationships with one another, have the same attitude of mind Christ Jesus had: who ... did not consider equality with God something to be used to his own advantage.'[1]**

## JEREMIAH 23:1–8

As I write, there are a number of significant elections and polls going on around the world, with leaders of various kinds seeking more power, longer power, or a fresh mandate. Leaders can have a huge impact on the people that they lead, but whether that impact is good or bad tends to depend on whether the leaders in question see their roles primarily in terms of the needs of the people they are appointed to lead or in terms of their own rights and privileges. Jeremiah puts those who are leading Judah as he writes firmly in the latter category. Their actions and decisions are harmful and even destructive to the people. They have failed to recognise that they have been called to be caring shepherds, serving on God's behalf those who are God's sheep. They see the people rather as those called to serve their leaders. Jeremiah knows, however, that God will not let this situation continue. He will eventually remove these upstart shepherds altogether and replace them with new leaders who really will have the needs of the people as their primary concern.

At this point, Jeremiah is given insight into God's future plans to send a transforming Saviour who will bring justice, safety and righteousness into the broken community. It seems clear that he is expecting that this will come at the time when the exiled community return to their homeland, but the New Testament constantly sees prophecies like this as fulfilled by Jesus, who is indeed 'The LORD Our Righteous Saviour' (v 6)! This passage stands as a warning not only to national leaders but also to any church leaders who forget that they are under-shepherds and see the people as there to support them rather than to be cared for by them.

**Reflect on any leadership position you might have, in home, church or work. Ask God to help you to be the kind of shepherd that he wants you to be.**

1 Phil 2:5,6, TNIV

 **BIBLE IN A YEAR:** Ezra 1,2; Luke 2

# DANGER: FALSE PROPHETS

**'Hear my teaching ... I will teach you lessons from the past ... tell the next generation the praiseworthy deeds of the LORD, his power, and the wonders he has done.'[1]**

**JEREMIAH 23:9–32**

The epistle of James warns that those who (presume to) teach will be judged more strictly.[2] The same clearly applies to those presuming to prophesy. It is so important that the name of God is not misused.[3] This could happen when the actions of those of us claiming to be God-followers don't reflect the purposes of the Lord we serve, but could lead watchers to think that God approves of what we do. In this chapter Jeremiah is looking particularly at those who claim that they speak for God, when what they are saying does not reflect the words or the purposes of the God they claim to be speaking for.

Before we judge these false prophets let's look at what they were saying. Basically it was: God loves you Israel, he has chosen you, therefore of course he won't let you be destroyed or exiled. They were absolutely right that God did love Israel and had chosen them. It was their jump to the 'therefore' that was the problem. They were filling people with false hopes (v 16), convincing themselves and the people that 'The LORD says: you will have peace' and 'No harm will come to you' (v 17), when, in actuality, God's judgement was about to fall on the people who had despised his covenant. It is very tempting for today's believers to say 'God loves you and wants the best for you', which is clearly true, and to follow it with a 'therefore' which says 'of course everything will turn out all right' – ie in the way we have convinced ourselves and them must be the best. It may be that we are right, but we need to be sure that we really have heard from God and are not just bringing false hope when we try to comfort people in this way.

**'This is eternal life: that they know you, the only true God, and Jesus Christ, whom you have sent.'[4] Thank you, Lord, for giving us your best!**

1 Ps 78:1–4, TNIV 2 James 3:1 3 Exod 20:7 4 John 17:3

**BIBLE IN A YEAR:** Ezra 3,4; Luke 3

# DANGER FOR GOD'S PROPHET

**'If their purpose or activity is of human origin, it will fail. But if it is from God, you will not be able to stop these men.'[1]**

## JEREMIAH 26

The book of Jeremiah constantly moves between Jeremiah's actual prophetic words and records of his life and circumstances. This chapter is mostly narrative and reflects some very interesting insights! First, Jeremiah speaks into a context where both the time - at the start of Jehoiakim's reign, only about 20 years before Jerusalem was destroyed - and the place - in the courtyard of God's house - is significant. Second, the reason the religious hierarchy at the time were so strongly opposed to Jeremiah was that they had identified God's interests with the existence and prosperity of the systems and structures they represented. In their view, God could not possibly be criticising these systems, so Jeremiah must be misrepresenting God and should die. Third, the strong anti-Jeremiah majority in government was not a unanimous one! Jeremiah did not stand alone. There were those, among both elders and prophets, willing to listen to God and to stand up and be counted as opposing the majority. Uriah, now largely forgotten, had died for proclaiming the same message. In Jeremiah's case the support of a few brave opposition leaders saved him from execution.

So what might this passage be saying to God's people today? First, when we speak out God's words, whether in gospel proclamation or challenge, are we taking proper account of the time and the place? Second, are we sometimes so sure of God's approval for our own systems or convictions that we have become unable to hear what God is actually saying to us and are therefore missing out on the possibility of transformation? Third, are we, like Gamaliel,[2] willing to stand against a religious establishment that is so sure of its own views that it seeks to condemn and destroy those who believe they are speaking God's words - without first actually listening to them!

**Lord, please keep me from being so sure of my own rightness that I fail to hear what you want to say to me.**

[1] Acts 5:38,39 [2] Acts 5: 33–40

 **BIBLE IN A YEAR:** Ezra 5,6; Psalm 77

# HOPE AND A FUTURE

**'You have been born anew into a living hope through the resurrection of Jesus Christ from the dead. You have a pure and enduring inheritance that cannot perish.'[1]**

**JEREMIAH 29:1–14**

There is no doubt that Jeremiah's primary calling was to the community remaining in Israel, specifically in Jerusalem, rather than to those already in exile in Babylon. However, that didn't mean that he wasn't also concerned about the exiled community. Our natural concentration on our own ministry doesn't mean totally avoiding involvement in God's other interests! Jeremiah could not preach to the exiles, but, as today's reading tells us, he could send a letter. The last part of this letter concentrates again on judgement, making sure that the exiles understand that those still in Judah are not exempt from that judgement, but the first part, which we are looking at today, is much more positive.

Verse 11, probably the best-known verse in Jeremiah, is often quoted as if it applies universally to every believer in every situation. However, it is important to recognise the original context. Jeremiah has two sets of advice for the exiles: first, advice about how to live in their present circumstances. Basically he says, settle down, get on with life and accept that you will be there long enough for your children to grow old. Then he turns to the future and God's promise that, after that long time, they will be enabled to go back to their own land. That is the hope and the future that Jeremiah is talking about. Jesus' prayer in John 17 makes it clear that his followers are not of this world, so perhaps Jeremiah's advice to the exiles in Babylon can helpfully be reinterpreted and applied to those of us awaiting return to our natural home in the new creation. We can't interpret verse 11 as a promise that everything will work out happily in this world, but we can be sure that one day we are going home.

**Try spending some time this week thinking about how your attitude to life now is, or should be, affected by your hope for an eternal future home.**

**1** 1 Pet 1:3,4, CEB

**BIBLE IN A YEAR:** Ezra 7,8; Luke 4

# AN INCURABLE WOUND HEALED

**'I trust in you, LORD; I say, "You are my God." My times are in your hands ... Let your face shine on your servant; save me in your unfailing love.'[1]**

## JEREMIAH 30

Have you ever, when travelling by train, pondered on the differences in the view depending on which way your seat faces? If facing forward, you see where you are going, if facing backwards you see where you have been. In this chapter Jeremiah seems to move his seat! He has been looking back at what has happened in the past – that is, Israel's total failure to keep the covenant – and turning slightly forward to what will happen in the near future – that is, God's judgement resulting in Israel's exile.

Now, however, he turns right round and looks beyond to the future where God will eventually bring healing and restoration to the nation which appeared to be fatally wounded. Parts of his message sound very like that of the false prophets. The difference is that Jeremiah's message of hope takes fully into account the reality of the people's sin and of God's judgement on them, which is both necessary and certain. Only when they recognise where they are now can Jeremiah point them forward to their future destination. The train is still moving, and he helps them to see that although the territory through which they have to travel will be unpleasant they will, by God's grace, eventually emerge into a bright and hopeful future. They will be enabled to return to their homeland and the covenant can be restored. The reiteration in verse 22 of the old covenant formula, when God says 'you will be my people and I will be your God', must have been a huge encouragement to all who had heard and heeded all of Jeremiah's words! One is reminded of the Good Friday call – today is Friday, but Sunday is coming!

**Jesus prayed that his followers might be with him, see his glory and have within them the Father's love and the Son himself![2] Lord, when I travel through difficult terrain, even when caused by my own bad choices, help me to remember my glorious destiny.**

1 Ps 31:14–16 2 John 17:24,26

 **BIBLE IN A YEAR:** Ezra 9,10; Luke 5

# THE ULTIMATE SORTER-OUT!

**'Let us then approach God's throne of grace with confidence, so that we may receive mercy and find grace to help us in our time of need.'[1]**

**PSALM 7**

I find this psalm really encouraging. It was apparently written in a specific situation when David was faced with a particular difficulty, but the content is quite general. We can't be sure what the situation was, though various suggestions concerning Benjamites or Cushites have been made.[2]

The focus of the psalm moves between the various circumstances that David had experienced or might encounter, his understanding of who God was and the interaction between these two things. David might be an innocent victim of opposition, injustice or violence, or he might actually be guilty of mistreating others in some way, but, whatever the circumstance, in all and every case David's God can sort it out. He can sort out David's enemies and if necessary he can sort out David! The reason that David thinks God is such a good sorter-out is that he has experienced God's deliverance, God's justice, God's righteousness, God's consistency. As far as David is concerned, God can be trusted to understand the situation, whatever it is, and to deal with it in a way that reflects his own character. He takes it for granted that God will be present with him, whatever is happening, and will act in wrath or mercy depending on the individual situation.

David's ability to praise God in all situations echoes that of Paul, who talks about his own contentment and the need for the Thessalonians to give thanks 'in all circumstances'.[3] In both cases the reason is not that God will take a particular action, but that he is who he is – and can be trusted, whatever we might think about the particular circumstances we are facing.

**'Now may the Lord of peace himself give you peace at all times and in every way. The Lord be with all of you.'[4]**

[1] Heb 4:16 [2] Cf 2 Sam 16:5–14; 18:19–33; 20:1,2 [3] 1 Thess 5:18; Phil 4:11
[4] 2 Thess 3:16

**BIBLE IN A YEAR:** Nehemiah 1,2; Psalm 78:1–37

# JOB

## NOW MY EYES HAVE SEEN YOU

The book of Job is framed by a prologue (chs 1,2) and an epilogue (42:7–17), prose passages which affirm Job's integrity. In the prologue we get a glimpse of the background to Job's suffering. This background is not known to Job and his friends, so a great deal of what they say is based on false assumptions. The main body of the book contains poetic speeches (3:1 – 42:6). Job curses the day of his birth (ch 3) and this is followed by three rounds of dialogue between Job and three friends (chs 4–27). Then, after an interlude (ch 28), follow Job's monologue (chs 29–31), Elihu's speeches (chs 32–37), the Lord's speeches (chs 38–41) and a final speech from Job (42:1–6).

It is clear from their debate that Job and his three friends presuppose 'retributive justice' – that only the sinful will suffer – which leads them to falsify either the integrity of Job or the integrity of God. Since Job suffers, his friends conclude that he must have sinned against God. Since Job finds himself innocent, his suffering prompts him to accuse God of punishing him unjustly. A key question 'Who has wisdom?' is raised on the issue of suffering. The debate in chapters 4–27 is followed by a wisdom poem in chapter 28, which ends with the conclusion that no one except God has wisdom. This anticipates the culminating Yahweh speeches (chs 38–41), where God's wisdom is revealed, following which Job himself comes to a deeper understanding – 'Now my eyes have seen you' (42:5).

It is noteworthy that the reader is directed 'from less to more adequate perspectives' as Carol Newsom puts it.[1] She further states: 'Within the dialogue, the friends' moral perspectives are shown to be inadequate by the compelling power of Job's words. The inadequacy of Job's perspective, however, is disclosed by the extraordinary speeches of God from the whirlwind. Surely one is supposed to adopt and endorse the perspective articulated by none other than God.'[2]

***Alison Lo***

[1] Carol A Newsom, 'The Book of Job', in LE Keck, ed, *New Interpreter's Bible*, vol 4, Abingdon, 1996, p337 [2] Newsom, 'The Book of Job,' p337

# FEARING GOD FOR NOUGHT

**'Search me, God, and know my heart; test me and know my anxious thoughts. See if there is any offensive way in me, and lead me in the way everlasting.'[1]**

**JOB 1**

Verses 1–5 provide the crucial information upon which the whole story is based. At the outset, the narrator describes Job as someone who is blameless, upright, fearing God and shunning evil (v 1). 'Blameless' (*tam*) highlights a person's moral character, conveying a sense of integrity. 'Blameless' and 'upright' are parallels and thus similar in meaning.[2] Being blameless and upright, however, doesn't mean that Job is sinless, because we all are human. It simply points out that Job is a person with genuine integrity. 'He feared God' underscores his utmost reverence toward God. To live out such an attitude, Job has chosen to shun evil as his way of life.

Verses 4 and 5 show Job's relentless concern and action to make sure that he and his family are right with God. The first five verses of the book thereby lay the foundation for Job's innocent suffering. Not only was he a righteous, God-fearing man, but his large family, great wealth and high status show how much he had to lose. His righteousness (v 1) is twice confirmed by God, using the same terms (v 8).[3] However, the motive of Job's piety is questioned by Satan – 'Does Job fear God for nothing?' (v 9). Satan suspects that Job's fear of God might be motivated by the divine blessings.

This question reminds me of the danger of preaching the prosperity gospel, which emphasises blessings from God – well-being, eternal life and so on. If this is the sole motive for following Jesus, our faith will soon capsize when we suffer adversity. Jesus never promises smooth sailing as he encourages his disciples to enter the small gate and narrow road, which lead to life.[4] Even Jesus' perfect righteousness does not make him immune from suffering.

**May Jesus examine our motives, so that we may follow him with a pure heart! May our love of him grow stronger when hardship strikes.**

[1] Ps 139:23,24 [2] Cf Ps 37:37 [3] See also Job 2:3 [4] Matt 7:13,14

**BIBLE IN A YEAR:** Nehemiah 3,4; Luke 6

# KNIGHT OF FAITH

**'In the mighty name of God ... We come; we cry; we watch; we wait; we look; we long for you!'[1]**

## JOB 2

Some people may find disturbing the image of God in the prologue of Job. Job's tragedy in chapter 1 reminds us of Abraham's test of sacrificing Isaac.[2] God saved Abraham's only heir - but he didn't save Job's ten children. Job's triumph in the first trial, however, doesn't save him from further trouble. The suffering of loss is followed by the suffering of pain. Now Satan afflicts Job with painful sores all over his body (v 7). Scraping himself with a piece of broken pottery (v 8), Job is tested to the extreme. The skin disease has made him unrecognisable (v 12).

From the human perspective, we could easily feel Mrs Job's frustration when she cries out to her husband (v 9): 'Are you still maintaining your integrity? Curse God and die!' Ironically, her remarks repeat God's affirmation of Job's disinterested righteousness after his first triumph (v 3). The Hebrew word *tumma* ('integrity'; vs 3,9) shares the same root with the key term *tam* ('blameless', v 3),[3] which describes Job's character. Mrs Job's question allows Job to express again his obedience to God's sovereignty - his power to take away what had been given and to strike with pain and disease (v 10).[4]

What would have happened if Job had listened to his wife? He would then have done what Satan had predicted: 'stretch out your hand and strike his flesh and bones, and he will surely curse you to your face' (v 5). Job's integrity and disinterested piety would have fallen apart, showing that if righteous people receive worldly things, their motives may become corrupted. Thankfully, Job didn't choose to curse God amidst his extreme pain. Søren Kierkegaard, in *Fear and Trembling*, considers Abraham as a 'knight of faith'. 'Yet Job excels Abraham' - as Newsom rightly puts it.[5]

**Teach us, Jesus, to persevere in faith like Job. May Job – 'the faithful par excellence' – continue to be an encouragement to us as we journey on with you!**

1 David Adam, *The Open Gate*, Triangle, 1994, p13 2 Gen 22 3 See also Job 1:1,8 4 Cf Job 1:21 5 Newsom, 'The Book of Job', p361

 **BIBLE IN A YEAR:** Nehemiah 5,6; Luke 7

# BE A GENUINE SELF

**'Hold thou my hand ... / No dread of ill shall make my soul afraid / ... and closer, closer draw me / To thy dear self – my hope, my joy, my all.'[1]**

**JOB 3**

Breaking a long week's silence with three friends, Job finally speaks up. Some people may expect him to curse God, but Job only curses the day of his birth (vs 3–10). In the prologue, the Hebrew word *barak* ('to bless') is used to replace the Hebrew verb for cursing when the object is God,[2] but here, when Job curses the day of his birth, the actual verbs for cursing - *qalal* (v 1) and *'arar* (v 8) - are used directly.

Why does Job wish to delete this day from the calendar? It didn't prevent him from being born to see the troubles (v 10). In his curse, he asks for the birth-day to be one of darkness and deep shadow (vs 4a,5). For the night, he asks for thick darkness to take over (v 6). He also calls for an absence of light (vs 4b,9) and joy (v 7). The wording 'Let that day be darkness!' (v 4, NRSV) sounds like a reverse of 'Let there be light' in Genesis 1:3, where God summons light on the first day of his creation.

Perhaps one may think that Job's utterance is not so very different from cursing God. Although it comes very close to such an offence, Job has never actually done so, at least not directly. We may also question whether Job's self-curse is consistent with his true faith. The confident and patient Job in the prologue has now become a desperate and troubled man. As Habel puts it, Job's curse 'falls on a past event, which would appear to be irreversible.'[3] That means it will never literally be fulfilled. Job simply expresses his pain by groaning about his devastating circumstances. Such innermost wrestling brings out another side of Job's integrity - being genuine and honest about his own feelings.

**Thank God for allowing us to be ourselves. Let's lay ourselves bare before him without denial – whatever feelings, troubles, deep secrets lie within us.**

**1** Fanny J Crosby, 1820–1915 **2** Job 1:5,11; 2:5,9 **3** Norman C Habel, *The Book of Job*, SCM, 1985, p107

# BE GENTLE TO JOB'S WOUND

**'A bruised reed he will not break, and a smouldering wick he will not snuff out. In faithfulness he will bring forth justice.'[1]**

## JOB 4

Opening the first round of dialogue with Job, Eliphaz's tone seems to be respectful (v 2), praising Job's ministry of counselling the needy (vs 3,4). Verse 5 reads, '*But now* trouble comes to you, and you are discouraged; it strikes you, and you are dismayed' (italics added). 'But now' implies that Job should apply to himself the instruction he has given to others. All positive comments only lead to a rebuke. Thereafter Eliphaz brings out the principles of retribution (vs 7–11) and human depravity (vs 17–21). This constitutes a theodicy – a way of vindicating God in the light of the existence of evil.

Regarding retribution, Eliphaz's focus seems to lack balance. By using the metaphor of preying lions to symbolise the wicked, Eliphaz puts more weight on their punishment (vs 8–11) than on the vindication of the righteous (v 7). Despite affirming Job's piety and integrity at the outset (v 6), Eliphaz eventually switches to casting doubt on Job. He then applies the theology of human depravity to Job (vs 17–21): no mortal is righteous from God's perspective (v 17). Even the heavenly beings are fallible and untrustworthy – so how much more are humans (vs 18,19), which implies Job's sinful human nature. Eliphaz points out that mortals will die '*without wisdom*' (v 21, italics added). These final words demonstrate that wisdom is Eliphaz's issue.

There is nothing wrong with Eliphaz's attempt to find meaning for human misfortune. However, it would be cruel for someone who is not suffering to stop a person who is suffering from speaking offensive words. Chapter 3 reveals how Job is struggling to come to terms with his faith. Eliphaz's theodicy aims to quench the uneasiness caused by Job's self-curse and lament. However, he overlooks and misjudges his friend's real need.

**'Holy and Strong One, in our weakness, we come to you. We bring friends in loneliness and heartache, in weariness and want, in fear and anxiety, strengthen us, good Lord!'[2]**

1 Isa 42:3 2 Adam, *The Open Gate*, p67

 **BIBLE IN A YEAR:** Nehemiah 9,10; Psalm 78:38–72

# NO IMPOSING OUR WILL

**'Make us, Lord, a sure place of your light, a sure place of your love, a sure place of your presence!'[1]**

**JOB 5**

Eliphaz's lecture on the human condition continues in verses 1-7. He then models for Job a doxology, praising God's power, justice and providence (vs 8–16). In addition to the principles of retribution and human depravity in chapter 4, Eliphaz proposes one more – divine discipline – which underscores God's loving chastisement on wrongdoers through discipline, to bring them back to him (vs 17–27).

When Eliphaz utters the doxology, he says to Job, '*But if I were you*, I would appeal to God [in my distress]; I would lay my cause before him' (v 8, italics added). Eliphaz demonstrates to Job how to cope with suffering. Then he praises God's great deeds: unsearchable and immeasurable actions (v 9); sending rain (v 10); rescuing and exalting the lowly and bereaved (v 11); thwarting the schemes of the crafty (vs 12–14); and bringing hope and justice to the needy (vs 15,16). Job self-curses and laments, whereas Eliphaz would sing praise. Advocating upbeat and triumphalist worship amidst dismay is unhealthy. As Brueggemann puts it, worship minus lament is finally 'a practice of denial, cover-up, and pretence, which sanctions social control.'[2] Lament needs a voice and it shouldn't be bottled up.

Eliphaz suggests that Job should submit himself happily to divine discipline (v 17), because it will eventually bring forth restoration and prosperity (vs 23–26), despite the pain of correction (vs 18–21). It implies that Eliphaz views Job's calamity as God's rod of discipline. He concludes, 'We have examined this, and it is true. *So hear it and apply it to yourself*' (v 27, italics added). He tries to impose a standard answer on Job. If Job had listened to Eliphaz, the motive of pursuing prosperity would have destroyed his integrity of disinterested piety. What Job desires is vindication, not restoration and prosperity.

**Do we treat our long-standing experience or belief as a model answer to others? May we learn to set people free instead of putting them into our boxes!**

1 Adam, *The Open Gate*, p62 2 Walter Brueggemann, 'The Costly Loss of Lament', *The Psalms and the Life of Faith*, Fortress, 1995, p102

**BIBLE IN A YEAR:** Nehemiah 11,12; Luke 9

# WHAT MAKES A FRIEND?

**'Give me a heart like thine, / give me a heart like thine, / by thy wonderful power, by thy grace every hour, / give me a heart like thine.'[1]**

## JOB 6

What does it mean to be a friend? It won't be difficult to find thousands of suggestions from the internet. In this chapter, Job lets us see what a toxic friend is like. In response to Eliphaz's remarks, Job cries out that the sheer weight of his suffering outweighs the sand of the seas. He complains about God's indifference to his anguish (vs 1-7). With no strength to cope with unrelenting pain and no hope for the future, Job urges God to finish his life (vs 8–13). Up to this point, he is trying to unpack his desperation – before venting his spleen on his friends.

What is a friend supposed to do when 'a despairing person' like Job is facing such crisis? We all know 'a friend in need is a friend indeed'. Job has the same expectation: '*A despairing man* should have the devotion of his friends, even though he forsakes the fear of the Almighty' (v 14, NIV 1984, italics added). Unfortunately his friends turn out to be as unreliable as intermittent streams which cease to flow in dry season, disappointing thirsty travellers (vs 15–21). A friend is supposed to listen, but Job complains that his friends treat his desperate words 'as wind' – something with little value (v 26). Instead of listening, they seek to correct and argue with Job without ground (vs 24–26). Job is even prepared to be betrayed by them (v 7).

It is so true that friendship is tested during crisis, as a familiar wisdom quote reminds us: 'You find out who your real friends are when you are going through a crisis. The ones worth keeping carry you through and the others fall by the wayside.' Actually Job's suffering doesn't end in the prologue, but his greater pain is yet to come as the friends rub salt into his wounds.

**Thank God for being such a faithful friend to us. Our friends may fail us, but you never forsake us!**

1 James H Cole

 **BIBLE IN A YEAR:** Nehemiah 13; Luke 10

# DIVINE-HUMAN SPLENDOUR

**'Nearer, still nearer, close to thy heart, / draw me, my Saviour, so precious thou art!'[1]**

**PSALM 8**

'*How* majestic ...!' (vs 1,9, TNIV) and '*what* are mere mortals ...?' (v 4, italics added) are the great exclamations in this psalm. The former expresses awe and admiration, whereas the latter expresses marvel and question. Schaefer rightly states, 'This awe and questioning is the distinction of Psalm 8 and the key to its interpretation.'[2] How is it so?

First, the psalmist is in awe of God, whose name and glory are manifested in all the earth and heavens (vs 1,9). To gaze at God's creation – the starry heavens in the night (v 3) – imparts an immense sense of human smallness. However, the focus of this psalm is not on the creation as a whole but on the place of humans within this creation. Verse 4 literally reads, 'What is man that you remember *him*, and the son of man that you care for *him*?', italics added. Humankind is so tiny compared with the enormous starry sky. Yet the Lord remembers and takes care of each individual human being – including me. How does this great Creator and Maintainer of the vast universe have time to attend personally to a tiny human creature? The overwhelming question 'what is humanity?' lies at the thematic centre of the psalm (v 4).

*Elohim* can be translated as 'angels', 'heavenly beings', 'gods' or 'God'. Because of an uneasiness with describing humans as God-like, verse 5a is traditionally rendered as 'You have made them a little lower than the angels'. However, the translation 'God' explains why humans are crowned with glory and honour (v 5b), which are divine attributes, and why they are endowed with surpassing power over the world (vs 6–8).[3] The psalmist is once again in awe of such a God who raises people to such high regard (v 9).

**The wonderment of God's 'making small humans big' surely awakens our deep-souled feelings of humble adoration to God. Praise him for linking his identity with ours!**

[1] Mrs CH Morris, 1862–1929 [2] Konrad Schaefer, *Psalms*, Berit Olam, Liturgical, 2001, p23 [3] Cf Gen 1:26–28

**BIBLE IN A YEAR:** Esther 1–3; Psalm 79

# QUESTIONING GOD!

**'O God, do not remain silent; do not turn a deaf ear, do not stand aloof, O God.'[1]**

## JOB 9

The imagery of lawsuits and the theme of God's power dominate this chapter. Hoping to sue God for treating him unjustly, Job questions how humans can win a lawsuit against God (vs 2–4). However, he finds it impossible to litigate against God because of his overwhelming power (vs 5–13,14–20) and his apparent abuse of it (vs 21–24). Lamenting the brevity of his life (vs 25,26), Job explores other options to resolve his situation (vs 27–35).

Here Job utters a hymn, bracketed by verses 5 and 13, with Job's comment on God's anger. At first glance it looks similar to the traditional doxology, praising God's might: overturning the mountains (v 5), shaking the earth (v 6), shutting off the light of the sun and stars (v 7) and creating the heaven, sea and stars (vs 8–10). However, the context suggests that Job uses this hymn to depict God's destructive acts with his power: violence without cause (vs 12,17,18), anger (vs 5,13) and perversion of justice (vs 22–24). Interestingly, verse 10 is almost identical to Eliphaz's praise of God in 5:9. For Eliphaz, God performs '*wonders*' and '*miracles*' to transform situations whereas for Job they elude human comprehension (vs 10,11).

Grieving the loss of his wife, CS Lewis cried out, 'Is it rational to believe in a bad God? ... The Cosmic Sadist, the spiteful imbecile?'[2] Without getting an answer, Lewis pondered, 'Can a mortal ask questions which God finds unanswerable? Quite easily, I should think! All nonsense questions are unanswerable. How many hours are there in a mile? Is yellow square or round? Probably half the questions we ask – half our great theological and metaphorical problems – are like that.'[3] Job's question 'How can a mortal win a lawsuit against God?'[4] is later proved by the Lord to be in this category.[5]

**Lord, when our repeated cries deafen us to your voice, calm us with your peace.**

[1] Ps 83:1 [2] CS Lewis, *A Grief Observed*, 1961, p27 [3] p58–59 [4] Berlin, Brettler, eds, *The Jewish Study Bible*, OUP, p1516 [5] Job 38:2; 40:2,8; 42:3

 **BIBLE IN A YEAR:** Esther 4,5; Luke 11

# UNQUENCHING DESIRE!

**'As the deer pants for streams of water, so my soul pants for you, my God. My soul thirsts for God, for the living God.'[1]**

**JOB 19**

This chapter is a lament, starting with Job accusing his friends of attacking him (vs 2–6). He also complains about God's violence against him (vs 7–12) and laments the alienation of his friends, kinsmen, guests, servants, wife and family (vs 13–20). He then pleads with his friends, stopping them from striking him (vs 21,22). Before giving them a final warning and rebuke (vs 28,29), he expresses his wish to have a defender to confront God for him (vs 23–27). Job's loneliness and helplessness are clearly seen. His misery and despair have grown.

A glimmer of hope sparks when Job explores the possibility of a redeemer to contend with God for him. Who is this redeemer (*go'el*)? We can trace the idea back to 9:33, where Job yearns for an arbiter to remove God's rod from him. Later, in 16:19, Job states, 'my witness is in heaven; my advocate is on high'. The 'redeemer' (v 25) here sounds similar to a hypothetical legal mediator of the arbiter and the witness. As Wilson puts it, 'underlying this picture of wanting a redeemer is Job's deeper desire for a restored relationship with God.'[2]

It is interesting to observe Job's inner perplexity and complexity. On the one hand, he grumbles about God's aggression: not answering his request for justice (v 7); depriving him of self-determination and dignity (vs 8,9); tearing him down and stripping his hope (v 10); treating him as enemy with anger and hostility (vs 11,12). On the other hand, he desires to rebuild his relationship with God – believing that his redeemer lives (v 25) and that he shall see God with his own eyes (v 27). It shows us the persistent spirit of Job – never giving up on his faith however low he is. It ignites hope in him (and us) to persevere.

**In the perplexity of life, may God protect our desire for him until we encounter him again!**

[1] Ps 42:1,2 [2] Lindsay Wilson, *Job*, Eerdmans, 2015, p107

# EYE-OPENING MOMENT

**'Lead me in your truth, and teach me, for you are the God of my salvation; for you I wait all day long.'[1]**

## JOB 38

The increasingly agonising pain drives Job into the dark valley,[2] where he demands God's response to his 'Why?' questions. The long wait triggers Job's final outburst: 'let the Almighty answer me' (31:35), through which he boldly challenges God to come out of hiding. Out of the whirlwind (v 1, NRSV), the Lord finally speaks. He speaks of his plan for the universe (v 2), with special attention to cosmic boundaries (vs 4–18), meteorological phenomena (vs 19–30,34–38) and a variety of mammals and birds (38:39 – 39:30).

Job has repeatedly questioned God's design for the cosmos, which seems to be chaotic and unjust. Interestingly, the Lord asks questions instead of answering. First, he challenges Job's limited understanding by asking, 'Who is this that obscures my plans with words without knowledge?' (v 2) – which Job later admits in 42:3. The unrelenting lists of rhetorical questions in the first divine speech focus on God's design. Do these questions only mean to belittle, rebuke and condemn the addressee? William Dumbrell concludes that 'There is no hint in these speeches that Job is being treated as a sinner; rather, he is being treated as one whose horizons need to be expanded.'[3]

Samuel Balentine rightly points out, 'God's rhetorical questions are a raid on Job's despair about what seems incomprehensible', serving to 'embolden a true servant whose faith is faint but worthy'.[4] It is noteworthy that God's appearance and his words are equally important here. The divine speech broadens Job's horizons, whereas the divine presence gives him a sense of closeness despite his overwhelming feelings of despair. Both signify God's approach to his beloved people – relationship building. Today we are so blessed to have both the Bible and the Holy Spirit within us.

**Lord, forgive us for obscuring your will and plan without knowledge. Remove our ignorance by coming to speak to us so that we may see things from your perspective.**

[1] Ps 25:5, NRSV [2] Job 3:11–26; 10:18–22; 24:1 [3] *The Faith of Israel*, 2nd edn, Baker, 2002, p258 [4] *The Book of Job*, Smyth & Helwys, 2006, p634

 **BIBLE IN A YEAR:** Esther 8–10; Luke 13

# THE BESTOWED CAPACITY

**'Those who hope in the LORD will renew their strength. They will soar on wings like eagles; they will run and not grow weary, they will walk and not be faint.'[1]**

**JOB 40**

The Lord concludes his first speech by challenging Job: 'Let him who accuses God *answer* him!' (v 2b, italics added). Putting his hand over his mouth, Job admitted his unworthiness and inability to reply: 'how can I reply to you? ... I have *no answer* ... I will *say no more*' (vs 4,5, italics added). We may wonder why the Lord needs to speak again after this. We should note that the same opening word occurs in the Lord's two speeches: 'Brace yourself like a man; I will question you, and you shall *answer* me' (v 7, italics added).[2] Job's silence in verse 5 doesn't seem to be a sufficient response, as he is repeatedly expected to answer God.[3]

God's second speech focuses on Job's justification of himself by condemning God (v 8). Demonstrating his governance of the world, God introduces the Behemoth (vs 15–24), a great beast which may be a hippopotamus, elephant or water buffalo. It does not matter whether the creature is natural or mythological – it mirrors Job in some ways.

First, Behemoth was created along with humans (v 15), which associates Job with the beast. Second, it is a creature with extraordinary power and strength, with bones like 'tubes of bronze' and limbs like 'rods of iron' (vs 16–18). Job once lamented 'What strength do I have ...?',[4] finding his 'bones' and 'sinews' not as strong as 'bronze'.[5] As Samuel Balentine puts it, 'If God has indeed made Behemoth just like him, then perhaps God has created Job with capacities he has not yet realised.'[6] Third, Behemoth withstands the raging river of Jordan and no one can tame it (vs 23,24). However, it doesn't pose a threat to God's created order. Similarly, Job's fearless courage to stand before God with unyielding faith and untameable strength is commendable.[7]

**Amidst adversity, let's notice the enduring capacities God bestows on us. May Moses' blessing to Asher reassure us: 'your strength will equal your days'.[8]**

[1] Isa 40:31 [2] Cf Job 38:3 [3] Cf Job 42:4 [4] Job 6:11 [5] Job 10:11; 6:12
[6] Balentine, *Job*, p684 [7] Balentine, *Job*, p686 [8] Deut 33:25

**BIBLE IN A YEAR:** Job 1,2; Psalm 80

# THE SUPREME OTHERNESS

**'He is the Rock, his works are perfect, and all his ways are just. A faithful God who does no wrong, upright and just is he.'[1]**

## JOB 41:1–11

Continuing the theme of his second speech, his divine governance in the world, the Lord displays another beast, Leviathan. He first challenges Job to contend with Leviathan (vs 1–11) and then depicts its physical characteristics (vs 12–34). Leviathan is sometimes seen as cosmic evil defeated by the Lord when the creation order was established.[2] In other places, however, it is considered as a valued creature along with other animals which God commended as 'good'.[3] Leviathan's evil characterisation doesn't seem to be obvious in this speech. Instead, it is described in a rather playful tone (cf v 5), so the meaning of this term is better left open for interpretation.

The Lord employs a series of rhetorical questions to challenge Job. Can Job catch Leviathan with a cord or hook? Can he domesticate it as a slave? Can he make it a child's pet? Can he…? Of course the answer is 'no' - there is no hope of subduing such an overpowering beast. Just as Behemoth is compared to Job, Leviathan is juxtaposed to God in verse 10—'No one is fierce enough to rouse *it*. Who then is able to stand against *me*?' (italics added). If Job is not able to capture Leviathan, how can he domesticate God by the retributive principle?

Everything in the world belongs to God (v 11b). Those who don't have the power and understanding of governing the universe are not qualified to question his divine justice, as it is beyond human comprehension. God is not obliged to pay back any claim against him (v 11a). Job's justifying himself by condemning God[4] is proved to be ignorant, as he admits in 42:3b.

**'As the heavens are higher than the earth, so are my ways higher than your ways and my thoughts than your thoughts.'[5] Praise God for his power, justice and wisdom!**

---

1 Deut 32:4 2 Cf Ps 74:13,14; Isa 27:1 3 Gen 1:21; cf Ps 148:7; 104:26
4 Job 40:8 5 Isa 55:9

 **BIBLE IN A YEAR:** Job 3,4; Luke 14

# FIRST-HAND EXPERIENCE

**'But if from there you seek the LORD your God, you will find him if you seek him with all your heart and with all your soul.'[1]**

**JOB 42**

This final chapter of Job first brings out Job's response to the Lord's second speech (vs 1–6) and then his vindication and double restoration (vs 7–17). The latter section serves as the epilogue of the book. Instead of remaining silent, Job gives a sufficient answer to God this time. His statement in verse 6, 'Therefore I despise myself and repent in dust and ashes', gives the impression that Job confesses his sin. However, the context doesn't suggest that God treats Job as a sinner who needs to repent. Job's obscuring God's plan without knowledge is no doubt corrected by God (verse 3),[2] but speaking of things without understanding them is not sin. Otherwise, the Lord will not commend him twice as his servant and as the one who has spoken the truth about him (vs 7,8). Furthermore, God designates Job to intercede for his friends, a gesture of vindicating Job.

It is possible, however, to understand verse 6 differently. (1) The word 'myself' doesn't appear at all in the Hebrew text. (2) The Hebrew *ma'as* ('despise' in NIV), used with an object, often means 'reject'. (3) The words *nhm 'l* ('repent' in NIV) can mean 'change one's mind about'. (4) The term 'dust and ashes' refers to mourning or lamenting and in this sentence can be taken as the object of both verbs. Thus, as Wilson suggests, this verse is best translated 'Therefore I reject and turn away from lamenting.'[3] Why does Job change his attitude? Because his encounter with the Lord has given him first-hand experience of God, surpassing all the second-hand knowledge he had in the past (v 5): 'My ears had heard of you but now my eyes have seen you'. Such a life-changing experience infuses new faith and hope in Job – he is no longer mourning and lamenting.

**Have you had a first-hand encounter with God recently? Ask Jesus to reveal himself. Be sensitive to the guidance of the Spirit and observe the change in your life.**

[1] Deut 4:29 [2] Cf Job 38:2 [3] Wilson, *Job*, p207

# DIVINE JUDGE-KING

**'Awaken me to your presence, Alert me to your love, Affirm me in your peace, Open to me your way ... For my heart is ready, Lord, my heart is ready.'[1]**

## PSALM 9

Psalm 9 uses rich images to portray the Lord, the most dominant of which is 'kingship'. How is it so? Appearing in the psalm as the king enthroned in Zion, the Lord is sovereign over all nations and his reign will last for ever (vs 4,7,8,11,19). One of the key roles of divine kingship is acting as the judge of the nations (vs 7,8). In the past, he has executed punishment against the wicked nations; their ruins have witnessed God's justice (vs 5,6). God has made himself known by implementing judgement (v 16). He judges the world with righteousness and equity (v 8).

This feature of divine kingship forms a firm theological foundation, on which prayers for help and songs of praise are based. For the Lord, as a stronghold for the oppressed, has the power and commitment to set things right in the human world, not abandoning those who seek him and not forgetting the cry of the afflicted (vs 9,10,12). No wonder the psalmist cries out to the Lord for deliverance from enemies (vs 13,19,20); and he summons his fellow Israelites to sing praise for God's acts (v 11).

This divine Judge-King reminds me of Jesus' parable of the widow and the unjust judge.[2] Even the unjust judge, who initially rejects the widow's pleas, eventually grants her request after she repeatedly pleads to him without giving up. How much more would our heavenly Father be compassionate to our cry to him in times of trouble? Jesus uses this parable to encourage his disciples to seek God's help relentlessly. The psalmist never stops pleading to God, even though he acknowledges that God is not always working out retribution immediately (v 19).

**'Will not the Judge of all the earth do right?'[3] May Abraham's conviction also be ours. Let's bring our pleas to our Judge-King and not be discouraged.**

1 Adam, *The Open Gate*, p17 2 Luke 18:1–8 3 Gen 18:25

 **BIBLE IN A YEAR:** Job 7,8; Psalms 81,82

# 1 TIMOTHY

## COMMANDED TO RESTORE

When he came upon the Ephesian church in disarray, Paul trusted Timothy, who had been ministering with him for over ten years,[1] to remain there and continue restoring it to health. Among other things, that meant: silencing those teaching false doctrines and their supporters; appointing new leaders in place of those deposed by Paul; unscrambling a messy situation over widows; and keeping himself on track while stressed and isolated.

1 Timothy is different from most of Paul's letters in getting straight to business (there is no extended thanksgiving). It also might not have been intended for reading in gathered worship, with just some sections to be shown to relevant people (eg 3:1–13; 5:7). The epistle has a thoroughly practical character. In interpreting it for our own times, we must keep in mind that it is addressed to someone having to exercise godly authority to restore a church to health: the 'letter brought the young leader instructions for providing first aid to a traumatised congregation - exceptional measures for a critical situation'.[2] Significant and unusually authoritative intervention has been necessary. We must take care not to normalise an abnormal situation. For example, the epistle recommends restrictions on our freedom in Christ for the purpose of restoring order (eg ch 2). We may ask, once order is restored, what next? Is the freedom in Christ proclaimed by Galatians 3:26–29 to be lost for ever because things got out of hand for a while in Ephesus?

There's a danger of using the text to answer questions it's not addressing and are way beyond its scope (such as finding a biblical basis for church order on three words 1 Timothy uses for leaders). Read in context, however, as wise advice for a church restoration project, we find - at least - the following principles that always apply: focus on truth; get people praying and listening to healthy teaching; appoint leaders whose characters have been tested; and work on arrangements that can be seen to be fair for all.

***Mike Archer***

[1] Cf Acts 16:1–3 [2] Gilbert Bilezkian, *Community 101*, Zondervan, 1997, p108

# COMMANDED TO COMMAND

**Give thanks and pray for those who raised you in the faith (v 2a).**

## 1 TIMOTHY 1:1–11

Paul, an apostle by the command of God (v 1), urges Timothy to continue his work of restoring the church in Ephesus. When Paul commands Timothy he uses the same word throughout the letter (1:3,5,18; 5:7; 6:13,17). Its root meaning is 'to transmit a message'. Authority is to be exercised by Timothy through making public commands in Paul's name, commanding false teachers to be silent (v 3).

Why is this necessary? Passing through on his way to Macedonia, Paul found God's household in Ephesus in a mess.[1] Key leaders have been teaching differently (v 3, literally), that is, not in accordance with the 'sound' teaching (v 10) that comes from the good news entrusted to Paul. Paul gives us few details of that different teaching. 'Myths' (v 4) may be idiomatic usage for far-fetched stories about the gods of Olympus. 'Endless genealogies' might refer to speculations about lineage from the Pentateuch, perhaps to justify a right to Levitical heritage[2] and explaining the desire to be 'teachers of the law' (v 7). The Law, Paul insists, has nothing to say to those made righteous by faith (vs 9–11).

This reconstruction is tentative, not least because a letter between two close friends assumes common knowledge and Paul doesn't spell this out. What's clear is the impact on the church: controversy, disunity and devotion to meaningless talk, rather than a 'stewardship of God in faith' (v 4, literally). Restoring this stewardship is at the heart of Timothy's commission. It might be best understood as pursuing God's ordering of things.[3] Sometimes there is no alternative: a line between truth and error has to be drawn, for to do anything else is to collude with darkness; no compromise is possible. Where might you be facing such a choice?

**Read Philippians 4:8,9 in the light of Paul's contrast between 'healthy' and 'diseased' teaching. What are you taking into yourself that's healthy and what might be less positive?**

[1] 1 Tim 3:15 [2] PH Towner, *The Letters to Timothy and Titus*, Eerdmans, 2006, p109–110 [3] Towner, p113

# ABUNDANT GRACE

**Review how you came to faith, asking God to show you how he was at work. Express your thanks for how his grace has been seen in your life.**

**1 TIMOTHY 1:12–20**

Having urged Timothy to pursue the 'stewardship of God in faith' (v 4, literally), which means resisting anything that does not conform to the healthy teaching of the gospel (v 10), Paul talks about how God's way of ordering things has worked out in his own life. He hints at parallels between his state before conversion and that of some of the straying leaders: he, too, was a blasphemer (v 13; cf v 20) and used violence in his persecution of the church.[1] What makes the difference is the grace of Christ: rather than rejecting Paul, as would have been deserved for such a sinner (vs 15,16), the Messiah, Jesus, saved Paul for his own sake and as an example of loving grace.

Not only did Jesus save him, he considered that Paul could become worthy of his trust, calling him into his service. What happened to Paul shows the boundless patience of Christ, that even such a violent enemy as he was could be reconciled to Jesus and receive eternal life.

There is only one fitting conclusion to Paul laying out the stewardship of God in his life: he is carried away into glorifying God for who he is and for what he has done (v 17). Even such a doxology still expresses a confrontational truth: the only way forward is proclaiming the gospel boldly, for the God who is known through the gospel is the only God there is to be known. The implication is clear: everyone must ensure that they are reconciled to God's way of ordering things, for everything else invites destruction (vs 19,20). Paul's story holds out hope for leaders who have gone astray - but Timothy is given a clear instruction: confronting false teaching is the only way of restoring God's household in Ephesus.

**We remember the utterly unexpected turnaround that happened when Paul came to Christ. Pray with confidence for God's grace to reach those known to you who seem far from Christ.**

[1] Cf 1 Tim 3:3

**BIBLE IN A YEAR:** Job 11,12; Luke 17

# RESTORING QUIETNESS

**Take some time identifying any controversial issues in your church or fellowship. How might God be challenging you to pray for them?**

## 1 TIMOTHY 2

Although Paul has other priorities here - particularly getting the church praying (vs 1,2) - we shall concentrate on the controversial verses about the role of women. In verse 15, Paul's focus seems to be the idle widows of 5:11–15. Lacking purpose in their idleness, some have strayed and are perpetuating the false teaching of the deposed leaders. As the culture then had few roles for women outside the home, Paul's point seems to be that remarriage and childbearing will save these women from idle purposelessness. Thus, childbearing is a means to restoring purposeful structure to their lives, thereby lessening disruption within the church. If that's right, then the heart of Paul's command is for us to live as purposeful, fruitful disciples.[1] Many will find significant purpose and delight in parenting today. Our culture now offers many other ways for women to express their calling beyond the home, but those who decide to concentrate on parenting should still be seen as honouring Paul's underlying instruction to be fruitful and purposeful.

Verse 12 isn't a straightforward command. It could be translated, 'I am not permitting',[2] suggesting contextually appropriate advice rather than a lasting ordinance. Given the continuing loyalty from some church women towards the deposed leaders who had grievously misled them,[3] they are no longer permitted to teach or enter into dialogue. The whole church is to be challenged to learn anew with a quiet, uncontentious spirit (quarrelsome men in v 8, women enjoined to 'quietness' in vs 11,12).

Remember that Paul's focus is on regulating this situation, not legislating for all situations always and everywhere. His concern here for the gospel, order and respectful relationships seems consistent with Ephesians 5:21; that is something that is applicable always.

**The mutual submission in Christ of Ephesians 5:21 is more taught than practised. Where do you need to grow in this area?**

[1] Similar points are made in 2 Thess 3:12 and Eph 4:28 [2] GD Fee, *1 and 2 Timothy, Titus*, Paternoster, 1995, p72 [3] 1 Tim 5:13; 2 Tim 3:6,7



**BIBLE IN A YEAR:** Job 13,14; Luke 18

# CHARACTER AND GIFTING

**Think of the last time someone challenged you about how you're living. How did you respond? Looking back, to what extent was the challenge justified?**

**1 TIMOTHY 3:1–7**

One of Paul's first actions was to remove at least two people from leadership in the Ephesian church.[1] It appears that speculation and lobbying began quickly as to who should be appointed instead (v 1). Paul is not offended by this, but he wants those aspiring to the noble task to know what it requires. He emphasises the kind of leadership needed to restore order and stability to a church that has been shaken. For example, drunkenness seems to have been a particular problem in Ephesus (eg vs 3,8),[2] so it gets an emphasis that will not be relevant for most situations. Likewise, the ban on recent converts becoming church leaders (v 6) would stifle many fruitful church planting movements around the world – perhaps the church in Ephesus was a case of once bitten, twice shy. The emphasis upon self-control and a refusal to get involved in angry, violent disputes again seems tailored to the context of a church that's been riven with quarrels. The need for restoration is never far from view.

Timothy is counselled to choose leaders who will quickly inspire trust, both inside the church and without, with Paul stressing character almost exclusively over gifting (the only exception being teaching). The goal is to settle the situation so that the church can once again grow and flourish.

Sometimes those with great gifts (especially when charm is added into the mix) aren't held to the same standards as others. Regardless of how great their gifts may be, leaders must be held accountable, for their own sakes as much as for the sake of God's household: anything other than this risks the good of the church and their own salvation (v 7). Character and gifts both matter, but in a restoration situation like Ephesus, character is the *sine qua non*.

**If you're in leadership, how are you accountable and to whom? For all of us, to whom have we given permission to ask us tough questions?**

[1] 1 Tim 1:19b,20 [2] See also Eph 5:18

**BIBLE IN A YEAR:** Job 15–17; Psalms 83,84

# TESTING LEADERS

**Leaders of all kinds are needed, in both the church and the world. Can you, under God's guidance, encourage anyone to explore leadership?**

## 1 TIMOTHY 3:8–13

Timothy is to put all who aspire to leadership to the test, examining their characters against the standards Paul has outlined. Only those proven to be above reproach are to be allowed to serve as overseers and deacons (v 10 in the Greek text makes no specific reference to deacons. It says, 'let them serve', the verb from which the noun deacon is derived. Thus, Paul is probably referring to both kinds of minister here). Clarity in faith and a commitment to upholding the truth is essential (v 9). Timothy is to examine them thoroughly, not being hasty to install anyone in office at this vulnerable time in the church's life.[1] It is debated whether verse 11 refers to the wives of leaders or female deacons (literally 'the women'). The parallels between verses 8 and 11 seem to suggest the latter (both verses begin with 'likewise', both are charged to be 'worthy of respect' and to be discreet in speech). Thus, women who aspire to be deacons are to be tested in the same way as men.

It is much easier to place someone in a leadership position than to ask them to step down. We get dazzled by the gifts the church needs, there are gaps to fill – and our needs sometimes overwhelm our caution. This letter reminds us of the damage that gifts without character can cause. It cautions all those with oversight responsibility to probe character as much as gifts. Verse 13 reminds us of what there is to be gained by testing leaders appropriately: great confidence before God (perhaps in prayer?) and a reputation in the community that commends the gospel.

The church and the world always need Christian leaders with grace, gifts and godly character. Godly character is the foundation, without which nothing is secure.

**Even Jesus needed to grow in wisdom and stature.[2] Where is God most at work in your character? And where might you be encouraging or resisting that work?**

[1] 1 Tim 5:22 [2] Luke 2:52

 **BIBLE IN A YEAR:** Job 18,19; Luke 19

# PILLAR AND FOUNDATION

**Today's passage includes a creed. Write down thanksgivings for how God has worked in your life. Say (or sing) a creed or credal hymn (eg Stuart Townend's 'In Christ alone').**

**1 TIMOTHY 3:14 – 4:5**

At the heart of today's passage is the confession in verse 16. In verse form, it has clearly been written in striking language to be used when the church gathered to worship. Paul commends it to Timothy as a memorable summary for the church to rally around and as a standard of right teaching against which other teaching can be measured. First, it stresses the humanity of Christ and the actuality of his victory. The first three lines affirm the reality of Christ's incarnation, resurrection and glorification. Then it daringly weaves those affirming their faith into the creed itself. The fourth and fifth lines stress the significance of the church's mission, as the gospel story preached to the nations, which has brought forth a harvest of believers in the world. We are all, Timothy is reminded, part of this story: a powerful thought to emphasise for a church shaken in its faith. The sixth line seems to refer to the ascension. Some writers think it refers to the ascension as the beginning of a continuing exaltation of Christ in heaven (rather than just the end of his earthly ministry).

Paul contrasts this with what the false teachers offer: world-denying spirituality that says 'No' to what God has created (4:3–5); deceit that comes from unholy spirits (v 1); and teachers who have as little sensitivity to what is right as badly burned fingers (v 2).

The reference to 'pillar' in 3:15 seems to recall the 'pillar of fire' in the wilderness which expressed God's powerful presence.[1] The story the creed embodies (the foundation) and God's empowering presence (the pillar) come together in the church of the living God (v 15), God's truth and power are expressed in community. Both are needed.

**To what extent in your life (or in your church) are power and truth equally expressed?**

[1] Exod 13:21,22; 14:24

# LIVING IN TENSION

**Thank God for when you've known him as 'a stronghold in times of trouble'.[1] Pray for any situations where you need to know that today.**

## PSALM 10

The Septuagint[2] has Psalms 9 and 10 as one psalm. They share enough distinctive phrases to suggest a single composition. Together they form an acrostic poem (where each two verses begins with successive letters of the Hebrew alphabet in turn).[3]

However, they are very different in tone. Psalm 9 confidently begins with praise for God's wonders (v 1) and ends with a plea for the Lord to arise and not let man triumph (vs 19,20). In contrast, Psalm 10 begins with a heartfelt cry: 'Why, LORD, do you stand so far off?' If God is a 'stronghold in times of trouble' (9:9), it asks, why do the helpless feel that he hides himself in those times (10:1)? A stark contrast indeed. The helpless are near despair, the prey of the wicked (vs 2,9,10), who boast that justice will never come, because God isn't watching (vs 5,6,11). This tension overflows into bold, desperate prayer: where 9:12 tells us that he doesn't forget the helpless, 10:12 demands that the Lord stir himself to ensure that they are not forgotten; where 9:16 tells us that the Lord is known by his justice, 10:13–15 urges him to put that into practice by breaking the power of the wicked. The wicked have reviled God (vs 3,13): the writer boldly asks the Lord to keep his promises and defend the helpless against evildoers (vs 12,15).

The two psalms embody different emotions, yet both are authentic responses to God. I remember a joy-filled church weekend at which God touched many, while I was wrestling with the news of one friend's miscarriage and another's diagnosis of terminal cancer. The psalms challenge us to be real *and* bold, living with the tension between the now and the not yet: grieving, yet not as those who have no hope.[4]

**Where is the wrestle between being real and bold most challenging for you at the moment?**

1 Ps 9:9 2 The Greek translation of the Old Testament 3 PC Craigie, *Psalms 1–50*, Word, 1983, p116 4 1 Thess 4:13,14

 **BIBLE IN A YEAR:** Job 22,23; Psalm 85

# GRACE ISN'T FAIR

**We received what we didn't deserve through grace and are expected to show grace to equally undeserving people. To whom are you finding it hardest to show grace right now?**

**1 TIMOTHY 4:6–16**

When facing any challenge, we have a choice how to respond. If we won't embrace what grace requires, we risk becoming embittered, angry with God and others, when we face difficulties. Even when treated unfairly, we still have a responsibility to respond graciously if God is to be honoured.[1]

Left behind to continue the difficult restoration work, Timothy could be forgiven for feeling overwhelmed and resentful at the task facing him. Paul is blunt: amid the pressures and the loneliness, Timothy must train himself to be godly, as diligently as an athlete trains their body (vs 7,8,15). The manner of life required by God's household applies to Timothy just as much as it does to overseers and deacons. If he is going to command and teach these things, he has to live them wholeheartedly as well (v 15), becoming a pattern for the believers – for then his relative youth won't be an issue. It doesn't matter how hard this is, there is no time for self-pity. He is to devote himself to reading scripture in the church, expounding it carefully, rather than engaging with false teaching directly (v 7): that's the restorative, healthy diet he is to feed the Ephesians.

In the midst of all these pressures and demands, Paul encourages Timothy: not only is he Paul's 'true son in the faith',[2] but they also share a hope in the living God. The one who has called Timothy to his service has gifted him in it (v 14) and is present with those who are faithful (v 10). Thus encouraged, Timothy is challenged to lead himself well through this time, keeping a gospel perspective on his struggles to ensure that he remembers what is at stake, both for himself and for those to whom he has been sent (v 16).

**Invite the Holy Spirit to show you where your perspective needs to become more gracious.**

**1** Rom 5:1–5 **2** 1 Tim 1:2

**BIBLE IN A YEAR:** Job 24–26; Luke 21

# SCARCE RESOURCES

**Pray that faith and generosity will be released among God's people.**

## 1 TIMOTHY 5:1–16

Caring for widows was an established practice in the early church,[1] but here there seem to be so many widows that caring for them all has become burdensome and controversial. Paul addresses the question first by appealing to family: as a proof of their sincerity as disciples (v 8), local families should care for their own widows (vs 4,16). Paul then allows that the church should support a widow (v 3) if she's without local family, of known good character and over the age of sixty (vs 9,10). Some writers identify a formalised order of widows to accompany the overseers and deacons. This seems to go further than the text justifies. What we can tentatively say is that a widow pledged not to remarry (cf vs 11,13) and, perhaps, pledged to devote herself to prayer and good works (v 5) was added to the list.

Being thus supported had allowed some widows to become unprofitably idle. Some had become pleasure seekers (v 6), while others were avidly meddling and talking nonsense (v 13). If the connection to promoting false teaching is here implied, 2 Timothy 3:6,7 makes it explicit: these meddlesome widows are involved in spreading false teaching from one church to another.

Having witnessed the impact of younger widows making a promise they can't keep (vs 11,12) and the impact on the church's reputation (vs 14,15), Paul tells Timothy to deny them support and challenge them to marry again. Withdrawing support is also commanded for the pleasure seekers, probably with the hope of drawing them back to God. As in Acts 6, dealing well with these difficult issues is crucial to restoring peace within the church. Paul tells Timothy to share this publicly (v 7) so that everyone may know that he is simply implementing Paul's instructions.

**Think of a situation known to you where resources are scarce and there's controversy about the way forward. Ask God to give you wisdom as to how to proceed.**

[1] Cf Acts 6:1–6

# ACCOUNTABILITY AND TRUST

**Pray for those who lead in your church. Ask God to show you how to pray for them in any private battles they may have.**

**1 TIMOTHY 5:17 – 6:2**

Restoring proper relationships within God's household is the primary focus of today's passage. Paul is concerned to restore a proper respect for those who hold leadership positions ('elders' in v 17 probably covers both overseers and deacons).

The removal of some leaders from office because of false teaching will have shaken church members. Their replacements have not yet been found and those appointed will find that trust is initially in short supply. Given this, Paul urges respect for those who preach and teach, an especially critical role as the gospel is once again proclaimed where false teaching has had a foothold (v 17). That respect should even stretch to the elders being supported financially as they give themselves to this work (v 18).

Given the troubles just past and the possible resentment at Paul's decisive action, Timothy is to be on guard against false allegations, perhaps from disgruntled supporters of deposed leaders: only a serious and corroborated allegation is to be heard (v 19). Timothy has to follow through on the other side of restoring trust as well. If he has to defend the leaders, he must also defend the people. If an accusation is proven, Timothy must publicly censure even the most significant of leaders: church members need to see that discipline will be applied to all, even to those Timothy himself has appointed (v 21). Church leaders need to understand that they will be held accountable and must honour the Lord in the way they lead (v 20). The requirement to restore trust in leadership in a church that has been shaken means that Timothy must be cautious in placing people in positions of authority (v 22), taking time over discernment, allowing the truth of people's characters to emerge (vs 24,25).

**We have become so individualistic that many struggle to be accountable to anyone. How is the need for accountable relationships expressed in your discipleship (eg small group, prayer triplet)?**

**BIBLE IN A YEAR:** Job 29,30; Luke 23

# DISCERNING MOTIVES

**Spend some time reflecting on the last time you were angry in (or about) church. Ask God to show you what you were really angry about and why.**

## 1 TIMOTHY 6:3–10

The last sentence of verse 2 belongs with today's passage in the Greek text. Bringing to an end the practical instructions on widows, elders and slaves, it introduces some reflections on the difference between true and false teachers. Given the warning that it takes time for the character of some to emerge clearly,[1] I think we should read these verses as aids to Timothy's discernment.

The healthy instruction that is the gospel comes from Jesus himself (v 3).[2] It is Jesus' acts and words that are the source of truth and the assurance of Paul's authority.[3] That is what justifies and grounds Paul's repeated assurance that his words are trustworthy.[4] If anyone teaches differently and doesn't assent to the healthy teaching that leads to godliness, Timothy is to disregard them.

These have been (and still are) the signs to look for in a teacher who is missing the mark: a proud assertiveness that doesn't submit to the gospel but gets drawn into wranglings and bitter arguments about words; a taste for controversy, leading to suspicious, malicious and envious attitudes; and a constant battle for their own way. They seek position and gain through being a church leader.[5] When you see teachers who are showing signs of this, Paul suggests, be prepared to intervene.

Although teaching elders have a right to be paid so that they can devote themselves to their duties,[6] where money becomes a primary motive all kinds of evil can follow (vs 9,10). Timothy must watch for this in himself (v 11) as well as others, seeking the true riches that come from being content in walking closely with God. Rather than finding such true riches, the false teachers have become lost.

**To what extent does a love of money affect your life? How might God want you to become more generous to others and trusting of him?**

[1] 1 Tim 5:24,25 [2] Cf 1 Tim 1:10b,11 [3] 1 Tim 1:1,11,12
[4] 1 Tim 1:15; 2:7; 3:1; 4:9 [5] Cf 1 Tim 3:3,8 [6] 1 Tim 5:17,18

 **BIBLE IN A YEAR:** Job 31,32; Psalms 86,87

# PURSUE GODLINESS

**Ask the Holy Spirit to show you if there's something from which you need to flee (v 11). If there is, ask God what you're to put in its place.**

**1 TIMOTHY 6:11–16**

So concerned is Paul about the dangers of the situation in which he has placed Timothy that he adds a fourth and solemn warning to stand against those teaching differently.[1]

Timothy has to thrust away from himself the diseased teaching (a better translation, suggesting its corrupting influence) with its controversies and the greed he has just been warned about (vs 3–10). He is to embrace wholeheartedly the course of life which grows Christian character. He has to live the example he is called to set,[2] being upright in his dealings with the Ephesians and reverent in his walk with God (v 11). Paul compares Timothy's struggle to engaging in an athletic contest (v 12),[3] challenging him to grasp the eternal prize that is his through Christ and which he claimed when making his 'good confession' (v 12). Made at his baptism, this is probably a renunciation of the lordship of Caesar (which might explain the reference to Jesus making a similar 'good confession' before Pilate, v 13). This eternal perspective reminds Timothy what is at stake and how much the struggle matters, to him and to the Ephesians.[4] Paul underscores this eternal perspective by making God a witness to the charge he is giving Timothy. He calls Timothy 'man of God' (v 11),[5] recalling the use of this term in the Old Testament, to underline his significance in God's plan. It is not just Paul asking this, it is also the God who gives life to everything (v 13), who is King of kings and Lord of lords (v 15).

This charge could be so overwhelming that it becomes disabling, but Paul wants Timothy to be in no doubt: his struggles matter to God. The God who gives life to everything is present with him, empowering him to succeed.

**Paul challenges Timothy to remember his 'good confession'. What public promises have you made to God? Where might you need to renew your commitment to them?**

[1] Cf 1 Tim 1:3–7,18–20; 4:1–7 [2] Cf 1 Tim 3:15; 4:12 [3] Cf 1 Tim 1:18
[4] Cf 1 Tim 4:16 [5] A term used of Moses, David and others; Fee, 1995, p149

**BIBLE IN A YEAR:** Job 33,34; Luke 24

# RICH IN GOOD DEEDS

**Thank God for those who have been generous and hospitable to you (particularly in church). In what ways might generosity and hospitality play a greater role in your life?**

## 1 TIMOTHY 6:17–21

Throughout the letter, we've seen the tensions around money in the Ephesian church: rich women dressing ostentatiously at worship;[1] so many widows receiving support that it has become burdensome;[2] the need to restate the practice of supporting elders financially;[3] and the need to emphasise that the right attitude to money is a criterion for leadership,[4] because wrong attitudes have led key leaders into losing their way.[5] Money is a divisive issue in Ephesus.

Paul commands Timothy to address the rich. It's a command because it's rarely easy to speak the truth to the powerful, especially when your livelihood may depend to an extent on their generosity. The wealthy possess not just money but influence. They're used to being listened to rather than listening. So Timothy is given no choice: he must do this. The rich are to be commanded not to be arrogant. It's a subtle temptation: when you're treated more favourably because you're rich, you can come incrementally to think of such treatment as your right. It's difficult for the rich not to become arrogant.

Timothy is charged to remind the rich that life always has an eternal dimension (v 7): too much trust in wealth risks undermining their trust in God, the source of all present enjoyment and blessing. They must use their wealth in a way that doesn't hinder their eternal calling (v 19). Cultivating generosity, being willing to share with the needy within the fellowship and being willing to serve in humble, shared tasks are all ways to ensure that God, rather than wealth, is their focus (v 18). Not only will this give them greater humility, but handling their wealth in a servant-hearted way will also reduce the tension around money within the church.

**Money can divide families and churches. Are there any areas in your life or at church where money has become divisive? Pray that God will show you the way forward.**

[1] 1 Tim 2:9,10 [2] 1 Tim 5:3–16 [3] 1 Tim 5:17,18 [4] 1 Tim 3:3,8 [5] 1 Tim 6:5–10

 **BIBLE IN A YEAR:** Job 35,36; Philippians 1

# STANDING FIRM

**Take time to name before God any challenges or struggles that you face, whether at home or at work. Ask God to show you how he is present in them.**

**PSALM 11**

In a time of crisis, the writer declares his confidence in the Lord (v 1). The threat seems imminent and real, compared to a startled bird fleeing from hunters and an ambush laid ready (vs 1,2). Trusted friends advise the writer to imitate the bird and flee. 'Look', they say, 'can you not see those gathering to ambush you? To shoot at you from the shadows, giving you no chance to save yourself?' The friends' concern threatens to overwhelm the writer's confidence in the Lord. After all, they say, when everything's being shaken, what discernible difference does one person's contribution actually make?

Having heard their advice and weighed it, still the writer takes his refuge in the Lord, who reigns both on earth and in heaven (v 4), both close to us and far above. His confidence depends not just on God's reign, but also on the way that reign is exercised. The verb translated 'examine' in verse 4 is drawn from the practice of assaying precious metals. Using the refiner's fire, the metal was melted so that impurities could be removed. Thus, God is not passively observing both the righteous and the wicked, he is actively assaying their worth (v 5). Those who delight in violence (cf v 2) will attract God's judgement, expressed as a dry-as-a-bone desert wind from which there's no relief and eventual destruction (v 6); but those who are righteous, purified through testing,[1] will know the Lord as their refuge and the privilege of experiencing God's empowering presence.

So the writer takes the Lord as his refuge, knowing that vindication will come to the one who puts their trust in him. As another psalm has it, 'Wait for the LORD; be strong and take heart and wait for the LORD.'[2]

**The promise is that we will see God's face. Ask God to show you any obstacles in your life that are keeping you from walking more closely with him.**

1 Rom 5:1–5 2 Ps 27:14

# MATTHEW 18:1 – 21:27

## TRAVELLING AND TEACHING

In these chapters we read about the rapidly moving events and the variety of teaching scenarios that Jesus encounters as his ministry draws to a close. Our readings fall into three sections: Jesus' private teaching to his disciples in Galilee (ch 18); journeying with the pilgrim crowds towards Jerusalem (chs 19,20); and his initial impact on the city (21:1–27). Jesus occupies the central position, with his unique, kingly authority emerging and shining brightly for the world to see. However, behind it all is his knowledge that his kingdom will only come through his suffering and death as a ransom for many.

Jesus' great skill in communication and teaching features strongly in these verses. He taught by using parables, dramatic actions, warnings, answers to questions and wise advice on dealing with difficult issues. His life demonstrated the qualities necessary to enter his kingdom. He had a rich life, full of people and relationships. Three times children came into the picture, as Jesus valued and blessed them. He deliberately stopped to heal two blind men. He would not compromise on demands for his kingdom, but took time to hear a mother's request and to challenge a young man to a life of discipleship. He skilfully responded to difficult questions from Pharisees, chief priests and elders, while demonstrating a thorough knowledge of the Law. He defended the nations' right to pray in the Temple and was unafraid to denounce its corrupt practices.

As we reflect on the life of Jesus portrayed in these chapters, let us be reminded of the humility of those who wish to enter his kingdom. Be enthused along with the pilgrim crowds to praise the one who came to bring salvation; learn with his disciples how to forgive and live a life of wisdom and purity; and let us tell our world the good news of its King.

***Sylvia Collinson***

### FOR FURTHER READING

Leon Morris, *The Gospel According to Matthew*, IVP, 1992

Tom Wright, *Matthew For Everyone* (Part 2), SPCK, 2002

# CHILD-LIKE LIVING

**Consider the children in your family or faith community. What can their lives teach about kingdom qualities?**

**MATTHEW 18:1–9**

Much in today's passage challenges our current church structure and practice. Churches and denominations give power to people with charisma, high levels of education, preaching skills, wealth, status or family connections. The kingdom of heaven has none of this. Greatness in Jesus' eyes is like a little child (not even an older one!). The lowly, insignificant one who is humble, trusting and dependent on God is truly great in God's eyes. That calls for certain qualities in Christian leaders.

Kingdom qualities which honour the King and protect the weak are often lacking today. Jesus said that if anyone causes even one little one, who believes in him, to stumble, it would be better if that person were dead. In the past, the general public trusted the church and its leaders to care for children, the weak and vulnerable. That is no longer true – trust has been betrayed by the many situations where those with greater power took advantage of 'little ones' (v 6). What a tragedy it is that governments have to legislate for the protection of the weak, even in church-run organisations! Now we must be trained to ensure that churches and Christian institutions are safe places.

We should ensure that our attitudes, values and behaviour – and what is considered acceptable in our communities of faith – do nothing to cause the downfall of his 'little ones'. Sin is a deadly serious matter, punishable by eternal fire. Godly wisdom, love, humility and courage are imperative for the people of God. We are called to deal with individual and corporate sin in our midst, starting first with ourselves, but for those who change direction and repent, the work of our Lord Jesus Christ on the cross, on behalf of all humanity, has made forgiveness and justification possible.

**Pray for yourself and for those who have leadership responsibilities among believers – for humility of soul, a servant heart, integrity of action and loving welcome for Christ's 'little ones'.**

**BIBLE IN A YEAR:** Job 39,40; Philippians 2

# CARING FOR LITTLE ONES

**'The Lord is my shepherd.'[1] Repeat this slowly, one word at a time, and meditate on its meaning for you today.**

## MATTHEW 18:10–14

Recently in Australia a sheep evaded shearing for over five years. It could barely walk under the weight of its fleece and when it was finally shorn the fleece weighed 40.45 kilograms, an (unofficial) world record! Sheep do not manage well on their own. They don't eat as wide a range of fodder as goats and they are prone to wander to places from which they need rescuing. They need a shepherd – just like the people of God, who are often referred to as sheep. Those who do not know him are as sheep without a shepherd. However independent we humans think we are, we all have a bit of the sheep in us. We all need the Shepherd.

A shepherd cares for every one of his precious sheep, however big or small. He takes the initiative: going out at personal sacrifice to seek the wanderers, to bring them back and to rejoice over their restoration. The Father does not wish any to perish. He sent the Good Shepherd to seek and to save the lost. The comment about angels in verse 10 has puzzled many, but we know that they also care for his little ones, 'so far as their necessity and situation demands'.[2] They bring their needs directly into the Father's presence.

We sheep can be responsible for mistreatment of others, like Ezekiel's fat sheep pushing and butting the weak, thin sheep.[3] Jesus warns his disciples not to despise the little ones who believe in him (v 10). The Lord and his angels knows if we lack concern for wanderers or weaker believers. We will be judged. We, like Peter, must feed his sheep and his lambs.[4] Pastoral care is both ours to receive and ours to give. Even in our littleness, we can share the Shepherd's love with others.

**Is there someone you know who needs to be loved, fed, cared for or brought back to the Shepherd? Make contact with them today.**

[1] Ps 23:1 [2] John Calvin, cited in Leon Morris, *The Gospel according to Matthew*, IVP, 1992, p464 [3] Ezek 34:17–21 [4] John 21:15–17



**BIBLE IN A YEAR:** Job 41,42; Philippians 3

# RESTORING THE WANDERER

**'Who is a pardoning God like thee? Or who has grace so rich and free?'[1]**

**MATTHEW 18:15–20**

This follows immediately after Jesus' teaching about the Father's concern for wandering sheep – and it may not necessarily refer to a breakdown in relationships ('against you', v 15, is not included in the most reliable manuscripts). The one who becomes aware of a brother's or sister's sin should go to them quietly and point out the matter, not with any hint of judgement but out of genuine love and concern for their well-being and that of the faith community. None of us is perfect: to point one finger at another's sin means pointing three fingers back at ourselves. Great wisdom, self-examination, unfailing love, prayer and the clear guidance of God's Spirit are required.

There can be no excuses for lack of action. The church has a clear responsibility to deal with sinful behaviour in its members. The name of Jesus is frequently brought into disrepute by the ungodly actions of his followers. Some may refuse to listen even when two or three witnesses, or the church as a whole, seeks to bring them to repentance – if that happens, they are to be treated as being outside the people of God. The church does not have the power to forgive or make decisions binding on God. He will only forgive when the offender makes their peace with him.

Verse 20 is often quoted when a small group gathers to pray and is certainly relevant there, but, in this context of restoring the wanderer, it applies to prayer for the sinner. The Jews have a saying that 'if two sit together and words of the Law (are) between them, the Shekinah (God's presence) rests between them.'[2] When two or three gather in Jesus' name, if they agree in prayer for the one whose sin is causing concern, then God's presence is with them.

**Next time you find yourself criticising another believer, think about your responsibility to them: should you pray for them? Encourage right behaviour? Or express loving concern?**

[1] Samuel Davies, 1723–61, 'Great God of wonders' [2] Mishnah, *Aboth* 3:2

**BIBLE IN A YEAR:** Proverbs 1,2; Philippians 4

# MORE THAN FORGIVENESS

**What has been (or is) the most difficult situation you have been in, requiring you to forgive?**

## MATTHEW 18:21–35

We believe that Jesus' twelve disciples lived in community 24/7 for three years. Perhaps it was like a three-year camping holiday with a group of twelve. Continually being with people is never easy. We know there were arguments and competition,[1] so Peter's question about forgiveness would have been very relevant. Jesus' answer far exceeded what the rabbis taught about forgiving someone three times: along with the parable that follows, Jesus tells us that our forgiveness must be limitless. Repentance and reconciliation are not prerequisites in order for us to forgive: we forgive because God has forgiven us an immeasurable debt.

These days we are more aware of physical and psychological abuse, unfaithfulness in marriage, bullying in schools and the workplace and many other situations where hurt and injury occur. Jesus calls the victim to the immensely difficult task of forgiving, even if the perpetrator is not repentant. Forgiveness then brings freedom to move on with life. However, along with Jesus' call to forgive, there is the responsibility of the Christian family and the surrounding community to provide protection and care so that the situation does not continue. Forgiveness is not a licence to persist in harmful behaviour – the offender may need to face justice.

The psalmist calls the people of God to 'give justice to the weak and the orphan; maintain the right of the lowly and the destitute. Rescue the weak and the needy; deliver them from the hand of the wicked.'[2] The faith community must not stand by and let abuse continue. Victims need to forgive, but the church needs to fight for justice for them. They, too, are loved by the Shepherd who wants them safe within his fold.

**Is there someone in your family, church or community who has suffered harm? How might you offer them practical love, protection and care, or encouragement to forgive?**

1 Mark 9:33,34; Matt 20:21 2 Ps 82:3,4, NRSV



**BIBLE IN A YEAR:** Proverbs 3,4; Psalm 89

# ONE FLESH, TORN APART

**'Love one another. In the same way I loved you, you love one another. This is how everyone will recognise that you are my disciples – when they see the love.'[1]**

**MATTHEW 19:1–15**

The deputation of Pharisees who questioned Jesus had no concern for people involved in marriage break-ups. Their question was designed to trap Jesus. In answering, Jesus referred to the original institution of marriage,[2] reminding them that one man and one woman leave their parents and are joined by God in lifetime commitment.

However, in a sinful world the ideal is not always achieved. Moses' law permitted a man to divorce if he found 'some indecency' in his wife.[3] This exception was debated by the rabbis, with numerous interpretations. Women had no right of divorce. Without a husband, they were destitute in a patriarchal society, so, for her protection, the law stipulated that a woman be given a certificate of divorce, giving her the freedom to remarry. The issue of divorce raises problems for Christians today. Jesus taught that there was only one situation in which divorce was permissible – sexual immorality.[4] Paul adds another: if an unbelieving partner doesn't wish to remain married to a believer.[5] That Paul made this further exception leads some Christians to find others – maybe violence?

In most churches and families today the issue is more than an academic dilemma. In addition to the actual couple, it affects children, parents, friends and church. We hold to the sanctity of marriage, but live with the reality of broken people and fragile marriages. We should make every effort to preserve a marriage, but if it is beyond repair, then those involved should be supported compassionately in their grief, in rebuilding their lives and, possibly, in their repentance. Children are often the innocent sufferers. Jesus' example of special care, loving welcome and tender prayer for children must extend to them through God's family.

**Give thanks for the stable marriages around you. Pray for those who are divorced or in difficult marriages. Can you support them?**

[1] John 13:34,35, *The Message* [2] Gen 2:22–24 [3] Deut 24:1, NASB
[4] Matt 5:31,32 [5] 1 Cor 7:12–15

**BIBLE IN A YEAR:** Proverbs 5,6; Colossians 1

# A COMPLETE TURNAROUND

**'For God is not unjust; he will not overlook your work and the love that you showed for his sake in serving the saints, as you still do.'[1]**

## MATTHEW 19:16–30

Recently some young, millionaire, business people engaged in a two-week experiment in Melbourne. For one week, in winter, they lived on the streets with the homeless and then in accommodation for the destitute. Suddenly they were struggling with preconceived ideas and the difficulties of a radically different lifestyle, safety concerns, hygiene issues and the futility of such a life. It turned their lives around – but it was only for a short period and then they went back to their former, comfortable living.

This young man who came to Jesus was impressive. He was diligent in obeying God's law and was seeking for something he felt was lacking in his life. Perhaps he expected to be given some outstanding action to perform. He sensed that Jesus had whatever he was looking for. He asked his question – but he was not ready for the answer. Jesus challenged him to sell all he owned, give it to the poor and follow him. That would involve a complete turnaround for the rest of his life; the cost was too great. Jesus challenged the very assumptions on which his life was built.

People without riches can easily condemn this young man, or the wealthy can say that God does not demand this of everyone – but what assumptions are our own lives built upon? We can cling to the security of financial independence, comfortable home and family, education, career or prestige, and fail to follow where Jesus leads. We should not be surprised when his call comes to us, as to the disciples, to leave and follow. It's a great reversal, but there are immeasurably richer rewards than in what we relinquish. Maybe we have turned from God's call with sadness, or our unfulfilled longings indicate we should turn from our securities and follow.

**What basic assumptions to your life is God challenging? You might discuss your feelings with a trusted fellow believer and pray together for God's guidance and strength to obey.**

[1] Heb 6:10, NRSV

 **BIBLE IN A YEAR:** Proverbs 7,8; Colossians 2

# PLEA FOR HELP

**'Do not be overcome by evil, but overcome evil with good.'[1]**

**PSALM 12**

I sometimes think our modern world is swamped with the words of lying politicians, a media hostile towards God's people, no one who cares for the poor or oppressed and little evidence that anyone lives a godly life. David obviously lived in a similar world. His psalm begins as a community lament. It does not express a personal complaint, but, in the light of the evil times, he pleads for God's help. He recognises that basic virtues like honesty, humility, compassion and faithfulness are no longer apparent. Instead, lies, flattery, boasting, wickedness and vileness are honoured by everyone. The mood changes in verse 5, with the assurance that God will arise and judge. He will protect. He will bring hope and confidence for those who feel he has abandoned them.

When we despair of the state of our present world and are tempted to think that God has forgotten us, this psalm brings a calm assurance. God hears our cries for help and knows when we pour out our hearts to him. He will arise to protect and deliver. As his agents, we also have our role in bringing virtue into this world: 'The only thing necessary for the triumph of evil is that good men[2] do nothing.'[3] It is no use withdrawing, or just condemning wickedness – we are to defend the poor and needy, and provide the vulnerable with safety.

Jesus promises to be with us always.[4] His promises stand firm and true, like precious metal refined seven times (v 6). God doesn't pretend evil does not exist. Jesus died for the sins of the repentant wicked. He came to 'bring good news to the poor … release to the captives … sight to the blind … to proclaim the year of the Lord's favour.'[5] That, too, is our mission in our time.

**How does today's psalm speak to your local church? Will you stand up for truth and righteousness, or defend the cause of the oppressed?**

1 Rom 12:21 2 [and women] 3 source unknown, but often attributed to Edmund Burke, 1729–97 4 Matt 28:20 5 Luke 4:18,19, NRSV

**BIBLE IN A YEAR:** Proverbs 9,10; Psalm 90

# NOT ARITHMETIC, BUT GRACE

**"Tis mercy all, immense and free; / for, O my God, it found out me!"[1] Thank God for his mercy to you.**

## MATTHEW 20:1–16

The chapter division between this and the previous incident is unhelpful. This parable further answers Peter's question on behalf of the twelve, 'We have left everything to follow you! What then will there be for us?'[2] Jesus assures them that they will receive eternal life and a significant place in his kingdom, along with everyone who has left all for his name's sake.

The landowner and the first set of labourers agreed to their payment for the day. Then, as the day progressed and further labourers were employed, each group was promised a fair wage. The last ones were just sent to work with no mention of payment. As in all parables, the emphasis falls on the last scene. The labourers who worked through the heat of the day had their expectations raised as they observed the others receiving their generous wages, but when they received the sum they had agreed, they bitterly complained that everyone was treated equally, no matter how long they worked. The landowner reminded them that their agreement was honoured exactly. His generosity was no reason for their jealousy. In God's kingdom the first will be last and the last will be first (v 16).[3]

The parable is for Peter and for all followers of Jesus, past, present and future. No one deserves God's salvation. It is not a matter of arithmetic, but of grace.[4] God is not answerable to humans for his actions. He gives his mercy equally to all who come to him. 'He who did not spare his own Son, but gave him up for us all – how will he not also, along with him, graciously give us all things?'[5] God has no favourite children. All receive salvation no matter how long they have been in his family. His grace is limitless.

**As humans and Christians, we can rate ourselves as deserving better or worse than others. God's mercy extends equally to all believers, even including the difficult ones!**

[1] C Wesley, 1707–88, 'And can it be' [2] Matt 19:27 [3] See also Matt 19:30
[4] Morris, *The Gospel According to Matthew*, IVP, 1992, p499 [5] Rom 8:32

 **BIBLE IN A YEAR:** Proverbs 11,12; Colossians 3

# LOOKING TO THE FUTURE

**'And being found in appearance as a man, he humbled himself by becoming obedient to death – even death on a cross!'[1] Meditate on what this meant for Jesus.**

**MATTHEW 20:17–28**

What a contrast! Jesus was looking to his immediate future, with its apparent powerlessness, suffering and ignominy, while his disciples had hopes of future power, comfort and glory! As Jesus journeyed to the Passover celebrations in Jerusalem, accompanied by his disciple band and their families and friends, he took the twelve aside to prepare them for what shortly awaited him in the city. Three times previously he had spoken of his betrayal, suffering, death and being raised on the third day. What little they had understood distressed them greatly.[2] This time he added that he would be mocked, flogged and crucified. He had spent three years serving humanity; now his hour of glory would cost him everything.

As Jesus anticipated his immediate future, James and John came with their mother,[3] seeking to shore up future positions of power, honour and glory in his kingdom. They wanted the best and, with probable family connections, they believed that was possible. She reverently requested Jesus' favour, to appoint her sons to the main positions in his coming kingdom. How must Jesus have felt? Despite three years of teaching, the nature of greatness in God's kingdom was still a mystery. What a different agenda from his!

As I dwell on the contrast, I identify more with the Zebedee family and the other disciples, than with Jesus. No one had learnt anything from the children or the young ruler. I, too, am influenced by ideas of importance, significance and achievement, rather than willingly accepting the lowly place of servanthood. To be honest, I recoil from rejection and suffering, but that's what being in God's kingdom includes. James and John would indeed drink of that cup. I, too, must embrace my cross and follow. That is kingdom greatness.

**Where is God calling you to servanthood? Give your fears to him and step out in faith. He holds your future in his hands.**

[1] Phil 2:8 [2] Matt 16:21; 17:12,22,23 [3] She was possibly Mary's sister, making James and John Jesus' cousins; John 19:25; Matt 27:56

**BIBLE IN A YEAR:** Proverbs 13,14; Colossians 4

# PEOPLE OR TASK ORIENTED?

**'There must be a beginning to any great matter, but the continuing to the end until it be thoroughly finished yields the true glory.'[1]**

## MATTHEW 20:29–34

Jesus and the pilgrim crowds were continuing their journey to Jerusalem. They passed through the ancient city of Jericho, with its palms and springs, and were preparing for the arduous ascent to Jerusalem. Luke tells us that Jesus steadfastly set his face to go to Jerusalem.[2] There was purpose in his journey. It was not just for Passover; it was the very reason he had come to earth – the climax of his life. Jesus would not be deflected from his destiny, so were these two blind men going to hold him up? He had a long day of uphill walking ahead. Some of us focus more on tasks than people. Jesus achieved the perfect balance between the two.

The crowd had no patience, but these blind men would not be put off. Against the odds, they took this, the only opportunity of their lives. Their cries increased in volume the more people tried to silence them. Their perseverance showed their faith in this Messianic Son of David. They pleaded for mercy, but when questioned, were quite specific, 'Lord, we want our sight' (v 33). The text says Jesus had 'compassion' (v 34). This term is never used of human concern. It is divine compassion for troubled people. Even in the midst of his own crises Jesus always had compassion on those in need.[3] Immediately, they received their sight and followed him, which probably indicates that they became his disciples.[4]

Was this encounter an interruption, or a divine appointment? To get the right balance between the tasks we have to perform and our Jesus-like compassion for people, requires wisdom and sensitivity to the leading of God's Spirit. We cannot meet every need, but love for neighbour makes demands on us, which we must not deny.[5] It may be the only opportunity those people have.

**What are your plans for this week? Do you need prayerfully to reconsider your balance between people and tasks?**

1 Sir Francis Drake, May 1587 2 Luke 9:51 3 Eg John 19:26,27; Luke 23:42,43
4 Mark 10:52 5 Luke 10:25–37

 **BIBLE IN A YEAR:** Proverbs 15,16; 1 Thessalonians 1

# A SEISMIC COMMOTION

**Play, sing or meditate on Handel's Hallelujah chorus: 'King of kings, for ever and ever, and Lord of lords, Hallelujah, Hallelujah. And he shall reign for ever and ever.'**

**MATTHEW 21:1–11**

Jesus and the pilgrim crowds climbed uphill from Jericho to reach the ridge overlooking Jerusalem. There he arranged a spectacular demonstration, to announce the true nature of his Messiahship. He deliberately prepared to enter the city on a colt which had never before been ridden (the presence of its mother would be calming in the noisy crowd), accompanied by enthusiastic, cheering crowds. This fulfilled Zechariah's prophecy, 'Triumphant and victorious is he, humble and riding on a donkey, on a colt, the foal of a donkey.'[1] The use of a lowly donkey, not a chariot or warhorse, signalled that he was coming in peace, bringing salvation.[2] His rule would not be achieved through military activity but through the suffering and humiliation of the King.

Cloaks were placed on the donkey and across its path. The pilgrim crowds and those from the city who welcomed him waved palm branches as they shouted and sang psalms of praise, salvation and victory (v 9).[3] Excitement was at a high pitch. They were proclaiming him as God's representative who would fulfil the hopes of their people. As the procession made its way into the city it caused a commotion of seismic[4] proportions. Everyone was asking, 'Who is this?' (v 10), to which the Galilean crowds proudly replied, 'This is Jesus, the prophet from Nazareth in Galilee' (v 11).[5]

The dramatic presentation of complex truth was a method used in the Jewish festivals, the prophets' messages and Jesus' life. This was a deliberate illustration of the prophecy of Zechariah. There was no longer a need for Jesus to play a quiet role. In this one action he allowed himself to be proclaimed as coming in the name of the Lord.

**Have you experienced truth conveyed through drama? Was it effective? How could you use drama to proclaim God's truth in family, church or community?**

[1] Zech 9:9, NRSV [2] Is 62:11, NRSV [3] Ps 118:26 [4] The city was 'stirred' (v 10, *seis-*, a strong word, used of earthquakes) [5] Cf Deut 18:15

**BIBLE IN A YEAR:** Proverbs 17,18; Psalm 91

# NOISE, SMELLS OR PRAYER?

**'Children of Jerusalem sang the praise of Jesus' name ... All unite to swell the song ... 'til hosannas fill the skies.'[1] Thank God, he accepts exuberant (maybe not musical!) praise.**

## MATTHEW 21:12–17

As the crowds entered Jerusalem, Jesus proceeded to the Temple, the centre of national and religious life. In the outermost Court of the Gentiles, money changers were exchanging (at a fee) unacceptable currency for high-grade silver coins required by every Jew to pay their annual Temple tax. Nearby were traders, selling, at considerable profit, unblemished animals and birds for the obligatory sacrifices to accompany the Temple rituals required after childbirth, healing or forgiveness of sin. The noise, smell and commotion made any attempt at prayer almost impossible. Yet this was the only place where Gentiles could pray and seek communion with the God of Israel.

No doubt the marketplace noise carried through to the Court of the Women, into which all Jews (except those with disabilities) could enter, and further into the Court of the Israelites where Temple services were conducted in which men could participate.[2] What was supposed to be a place of prayer and worship for all nations was no better than a den of robbers.[3] Jesus' righteous indignation was not an aberration: he was claiming his rightful authority to deal with sin at the heart of his nation. By his death he would shortly open up the way for all nations to access the Father. This was a symbolic first step.

Many from the crowds were still with him, no doubt observing his actions with delight! The excitement of their children had not dissipated; among the marketplace noise they continued shouting, 'Hosanna to the Son of David'. This was more than the authorities could stomach. When they indignantly approached Jesus to reproach them, he questioned their knowledge of the Scriptures, recalling that children's praise is always accepted.[4] Jesus would not be bullied. Authority, justice and judgement are in his hands.

**What practical steps could your church make to enable men, women and children of all nations (and abilities) to better encounter God?**

[1] J Henley, 1800–42 [2] William Barclay, *Gospel of Matthew*, Vol 2, p268–71
[3] Is 56:7; Jer 7:11 [4] Ps 8:2

 **BIBLE IN A YEAR:** Proverbs 19,20; 1 Thessalonians 2

# SNAKES AND DOVES

**'Do not claim to be wiser than you are. Do not repay anyone evil for evil, but take thought for what is noble in the sight of all.'[1]**

**MATTHEW 21:18–27**

In Jesus' time most people ate two meals a day – and maybe an early snack. Jesus and his disciples left early for the Temple. Being hungry, he looked for figs on a roadside tree, but there was nothing, not even the first, unpalatable crop. The prophet Micah[2] likened Israel's moral and religious failure to that of a fig tree with no fruit. Thus, by cursing the fig tree, Jesus was indicating the judgement which would come on the fruitless, religious practices of Judaism.

However, the disciples responded not to the judgement symbolism but to the impressive power of Jesus' word. Their question facilitated his teaching about prayer with undoubting faith. His promise concerning prayer does not mean that we can 'believe six impossible things before breakfast'[3] and God will answer. Praying with faith is not bending God to what we want, but confident trust in him to answer for good in all circumstances.

The crowds also went to the Temple early each morning, to hear Jesus teach.[4] No wonder the chief priests and elders challenged his popularity, questioning the source of his authority. Whatever answer he gave would cause his arrest, but Jesus would not be trapped. He turned their enquiry back onto them and questioned them on John the Baptist's authority. They refused to answer him. Neither would he answer them. Dealing with both supporters and opposition, Jesus was our perfect example of being 'wise as serpents and innocent as doves'.[5] We need to be both, to serve him well. Prayer for wisdom will be answered generously.[6] Perhaps harmless/innocent as doves is more difficult to understand. Innocence is not the same as naivety – innocence knows the full depths of evil, but is not part of it.

**Pray for Christians in leadership positions in church or community and for yourself, that God will enable wisdom like serpents and innocence like doves. Trust him to answer.**

[1] Rom 12:16,17, NRSV [2] Mic 7:1 [3] Lewis Carroll, *Alice through the Looking Glass* [4] Luke 21:38 [5] Matt 10:16, NRSV [6] James 1:5,6

**BIBLE IN A YEAR:** Proverbs 21,22; 1 Thessalonians 3

# PRAYER FOR DELIVERANCE

**'Through all the changing scenes of life, / in trouble and in joy, / the praises of my God shall still / my heart and tongue employ.'[1]**

## PSALM 13

David is desolate. He feels abandoned, forgotten by the Lord, the one who is in covenant relationship with his people Israel. However, because of that relationship, he can address his misery to him. Four times he asks the Lord, 'How long?' The martyrs prayed the same prayer, 'Sovereign Lord, holy and true, how long will it be before you judge and avenge our blood on the inhabitants of the earth?'[2] How many times have we expressed the same to God? We know he has the power to lovingly deliver his beloved people from evil and yet he seems to do nothing. David's despair is compounded because he is tormented day and night by his own thoughts and by his enemy exalting over him. Ultimately, God doesn't answer human questions. He dwells in eternity and is not confined to time. He will act, but only when it is right.

So David asks that his eyes will be opened, for he fears that without God's intervention he may well die at the hands of his enemy. Then, although the circumstances have not changed, he confidently affirms his trust in the steadfast, covenant, faithfulness of the Lord and rejoices in the hope of salvation which God has so bountifully given his people.

Under the new covenant, we receive his steadfast, unfailing love, but there are times when we, too, may feel deserted by God. Some call it 'the dark night of the soul'. David's words encourage us to tell God honestly, to ask for our eyes to be enlightened and consciously to place our confidence in his unfailing love. Nothing may change, except us, but we will find reason to rejoice and praise him for his goodness, for, as verse 6 states, he has dealt bountifully with us, granting our God-inspired desires.

**Are you, or someone you know, feeling that God is not listening? Pray for patience and for eyes to see his steadfast, bountiful, covenant love within the circumstances.**

[1] Nahum Tate, 1652–1715, and Nicholas Brady, 1659–1726 [2] Rev 6:10, NRSV



**BIBLE IN A YEAR:** Proverbs 23,24; Psalms 92,93

Scripture Union
THE GOOD NEWS FUND

# 1 CHRONICLES 10–29

## THE MEASURE OF A KING

In the Hebrew Bible, 1 and 2 Chronicles were originally a single book called 'The Matters of the Days', comprising material also found in 2 Samuel and 1 and 2 Kings. It was divided in two in the Greek version of the Old Testament, called the Septuagint (c 200 BC). Its Greek name, *I & II Paralipomenon*, meaning 'The Things Omitted', referred to details not related in 2 Samuel and 1 Kings. The title 'Chronicles' originated with Jerome's Latin Vulgate translation (c AD 400).

Jewish tradition identifies the author (known to Bible scholars as 'the Chronicler') as Ezra, who is associated also with the books of Ezra and Nehemiah. The priest and scribe Ezra led the second group of Jews returning from Babylon to Jerusalem in the mid-fifth century BC. We cannot be sure whether Ezra was indeed the author, but the Chronicler certainly does view Israel's and Judah's history from a priestly perspective. This explains his emphasis on the importance of obeying the Law and worshipping the Lord appropriately. Kings are measured and appraised according to their observance of these things. The Temple, in its preparation under David and its construction under Solomon, takes on huge significance. All of this indicates the Chronicler's concern not merely to give a historical account but also to show the right path that leads to blessing.

It seems most likely that Chronicles was written to encourage the Jews who had returned to Judah after the Exile and those still dispersed throughout the Persian Empire. Judah was no longer a kingdom with its own king. The Exile had been an extremely difficult learning curve. The Jews needed reminding about their history in a way that would help them steer away from the sins that had led to the kingdom's demise, while filling them with hope for the future blessing God had promised through David's messianic descendant. Jesus Christ is not mentioned by name, but his presence is prefigured in the godly kings and priests commended by the Chronicler.

***Andrew Heron***

# DISASTROUS DISOBEDIENCE

**'It is a dreadful thing to fall into the hands of the living God.'[1]**

**1 CHRONICLES 10**

In our introduction to 1 Chronicles, we noted that the author gives us a religious or spiritual interpretation of events in the days of Israel's kings. This leads him to concentrate on David and his establishment of Jerusalem as capital of a united Israel. He focuses eventually on Solomon's Temple and its importance at the centre of religious life. Nevertheless, it comes as rather a surprise to the modern reader that Israel's first king, David's predecessor Saul, is allotted only one short chapter - and that one chapter does not even attempt to give a summary of Saul's 40-year reign. It merely relates the circumstances of his death and the end of his royal line. As far as the Chronicler is concerned, Saul clearly had nothing to commend him.

Chapter 10 certainly presents Saul in a very poor light. This comes in contrast with other people mentioned in the passage. While not condoning suicide, the Chronicler appears to commend Saul's armour-bearer for falling on his sword and thus remaining faithful to his master. More clearly, the author extols the 'valiant men' of Jabesh Gilead for their courage in rescuing Saul's and his sons' remains from further humiliation in death (vs 11,12). How faithful and courageous are we Christians in our divine King's service?

Nothing, however, is said to redeem Saul's character. His downfall is clearly explained as a warning to us in verses 13 and 14. Refusal to obey God's word - notably, dabbling in the occult - brought about his demise and the end of his dynasty at God's own hand. The New Testament similarly relates the death of Ananias and Sapphira[2] to avert us from the danger of deliberate disobedience to God and his word. Are we taking heed?

**'We cannot rely on God's promises without obeying his commandments.'[3] Thank God now for his promises and ask for grace to obey his word.**

[1] Heb 10:31 [2] Acts 5:1–11 [3] John Calvin, 1509–64

# A TYPE OF CHRIST

**David pre-figures his greatest descendant, Jesus Christ, albeit imperfectly. How much is your life a reflection of your Lord and Saviour?**

## 1 CHRONICLES 11:1–9

The focus now switches to David and his descendants. Nothing is said about the short rule of Saul's son Ish-Bosheth.[1] Nor is any mention made of David's seven-year reign over Judah in Hebron – an example of the Chronicler's omission of events which the books of Samuel and Kings relate in detail. These omissions explain why the Ancient Greek version of the Old Testament, the Septuagint (written for Greek-speaking Jews of the Diaspora) titled this book 'Things left out' (*Paralipomenon*)!

David is presented as God's chosen successor to the throne vacated by the unworthy Saul. David is elsewhere described as 'a man after [the Lord's] own heart'[2] and his accession is described in terms that speak to Christians of their beloved King, David's divine descendant.

All Israel gathers around David as their 'own flesh and blood' (v 1). King Jesus is not ashamed to call those he has redeemed his 'brothers and sisters'![3] The Israelites recognise David as the one whose leadership delivered them from enemy hands, even during Saul's reign (v 2). Who is the one who rescues me from this body that is subject to death? Romans 7:25 gives the answer: 'Thanks be to God, who delivers me through Jesus Christ our Lord!' The people acknowledge David as Israel's shepherd and ruler (v 2); David's royal line will produce a successor who calls himself 'the good shepherd'.[4] David made a covenant with the elders of Israel at Hebron (v 3); David's descendant is the mediator of a superior covenant, sealed by his own blood.[5] David was Israel's anointed king (v 3); Acts 10:38 tells us 'God anointed Jesus of Nazareth with the Holy Spirit and power'. No wonder a well-known hymn about Jesus ends each verse with, 'Hallelujah! What a Saviour!'[6]

**Look up and quietly meditate upon the words of Philip P Bliss' great hymn, 'Man of Sorrows'.**

1 2 Sam 2–4 2 1 Sam 13:14 3 Heb 2:11 4 John 10:11 5 Heb 8:6; Luke 22:20
6 PP Bliss, 1838–76, 'Man of sorrows'

 **BIBLE IN A YEAR:** Proverbs 27,28; 1 Thessalonians 5

# A WRONG MOVE

**Lord, let me not lean on my own understanding, but submit to you in all my ways, that you may make my paths straight![1]**

## 1 CHRONICLES 13

The Ark of the Covenant was God's meeting place with the Israelites and the symbol of his holy presence among them. The Philistines had captured and held it for seven months after winning the battle of Aphek.[2] Eventually it had been entrusted to Abinadab of Kiriath Jearim.[3] There it spent a large number of years until David decided to bring it to his new capital, Jerusalem.

God's outburst of anger against Abinadab's son, Uzzah, appears excessively harsh to the modern eye. Why should the simple act of reaching out to steady the Ark have cost him his life? Uzzah's gesture was, in fact, the last of several serious errors that violated God's holiness. To start with, David's decision to move the Ark is taken after consultation with his army officers. He should have first discussed his plan with the priests and Levites who were, by law, the ark's designated guardians. Second, the Ark was only ever to be transported on the shoulders of Levites of the Kohathite clan.[4] David chose to move it on an ox-drawn cart, which was an improper way of carrying the sacred item. Third, no human hand was to touch the ark.[5] Uzzah failed to obey God's strict command. Immediate death was the consequence.

There is, however, possibly a fourth error which may have cost Uzzah his life, as a warning sign to others. During the time the Ark had stayed in his father Abinadab's house, Uzzah had perhaps become overfamiliar with this most holy object. Reaching out his hand to touch the Ark showed a lack of respect for God's revealed way of doing things. In our relationship with God, we need to avoid overfamiliarity with the Most High!

**Pray for wisdom to know how to cultivate a close, intimate relationship with God while maintaining a deep reverence for his holiness.**

[1] Cf Prov 3:5,6 [2] 1 Sam 4:1–11 [3] 1 Sam 7:1,2 [4] Num 7:1–9 [5] Num 4:15

**BIBLE IN A YEAR:** Proverbs 29,30; 2 Thessalonians 1

# A GOD OF SECOND CHANCES

**Unlike Saul, David learned from his mistakes and humbly accepted God's correction. As a follower of Christ, do you humbly submit to your Master's discipline?!**

## 1 CHRONICLES 15:1–16

'God's work done in God's way will never lack God's supplies.' This was declared by a man who knew what he was talking about – Hudson Taylor, the 19th-century pioneering missionary to inland China. Through his tireless ministry, hundreds of missionaries were inspired to serve God in China. Schools were founded, preaching stations opened and national workers raised up. The term 'successful' is certainly true of this passionate Yorkshireman, whose consecration and obedience to God are inspirational.

Does our consecration and obedience to God necessarily make us 'successful'? Hudson Taylor's life seems to say 'Yes!' – as do the events of today's passage, in which King David learns from his disastrous mistakes in chapter 13 and goes on successfully to bring the Ark of the Covenant to Jerusalem. David himself admits why his first attempt had been such a dismal failure: 'We did not enquire of [God] about how to do it in the prescribed way' (v 13).

David's second attempt, carried out according to God's own instructions, in compliance with God's own way, leads to a much happier result than his first. This is something Hudson Taylor knew all about from his own experience nearly three thousand years later. Yet Taylor's 'success' was not gained without much personal sacrifice, for during his exemplary missionary career he was beaten, robbed and ridiculed, and he buried two wives and six children. Let us be certain of this: God is no man's debtor. We do not receive his favour in return for our good works. All is entirely of his grace. Yet, he delights to reward our faithful and obedient service. What greater reward can there be than his 'Well done, good and faithful servant!'?[1]

**Do you know someone discouraged by some recent moral failure? Look for ways to encourage that person to trust God for forgiveness and strength to repent and start afresh.**

1 Matt 25:21,23



**BIBLE IN A YEAR:** Proverbs 31; Psalm 94

# AN AUDIENCE OF ONE

**'God is most glorified in us when we are most satisfied in him.'[1]**

**1 CHRONICLES 15:25 – 16:6**

The symbol of God's presence and glory among the Israelites now finally rests at the heart of national life, after its many years of nomadic wandering. Obedient observance of God's instructions for transporting the Ark of the Covenant makes this a day to be remembered. It is an occasion of abundant joy, producing overflowing generosity. The spirit of adoration and thanksgiving which characterises this day leads David to establish an enduring institution of worship, involving the Levites as its consecrated leaders. David's own words in Psalm 22:3 encourage us to believe that God is wonderfully present in the midst of his worshipping community: 'You are holy, enthroned on the praises of Israel' (NRSV).

David himself provides a model of what uninhibited joy in worship can look like. His exuberant dancing and celebrating may not have pleased his wife Michal (v 29), but David is not concerned if people think he is undignified. His audience is the Lord. Why should he (we?) worry about what others think, if God is truly central to his (our) worship? As worshippers of the true, living God, how does our enthusiasm compare with the often wild excitement of those who adore the gods of the football stadium or the rock arena?

David's joyful exuberance before God is not the selfish action of a mere attention-grabber or thrill-seeker! It issues in remarkable generosity towards others. After providing all that was necessary for the appropriate burnt offerings and fellowship offerings, David sends the worshippers away, both male and female (not only the men, who were traditionally the heads of their households) with delicious food for their own personal enjoyment. Genuine worship fills us with joy in and from God that leads us to be generous towards others, as God has been generous towards us.

**Reflect on Philippians 4:4: 'Rejoice in the Lord always. I will say it again: rejoice!' Do people around you see your joy in God and benefit from it?**

[1] John Piper, b1946

# THE ONE TRUE GOD

**The first commandment says: 'You shall have no other gods before me'.[1] What rivals does he have in your life?**

## 1 CHRONICLES 16:7–36

On the day David sets the Ark of the Covenant in its resting place in Jerusalem, Asaph and his Levite associates lead the gathered assembly in a hymn of praise. That hymn is a medley of verses drawn from Psalms 105, 96 and 106. It takes up the theme of praise to the Lord. Part 1 (vs 8–22) calls on God's covenant people to ascribe greatness to the Lord. Part 2 (vs 23–33) commands the Gentile nations to acknowledge the Lord's supremacy. Part 3 is a great closing 'Hosanna', praising God for his salvation.

Part 2 invites the nations to compare their gods with Israel's God. In verse 26, the 'gods' of the nations are called 'idols' (Hebrew, *elilim*).The root meaning of *elilim* conveys the idea of insufficiency or worthlessness. Most English Bibles translate this word as 'idols'. This may give the modern reader the impression that the gods worshipped by the nations were not real, but merely wooden or stone effigies carved by human hand. That is far from true. The Bible makes clear that fallen spiritual beings really do exist and have the power to lead their worshippers away from the one, true God. Indeed, the apostle Paul calls Satan 'the god of this world'.[2]

David's song shows us that the Lord is truly worthy of the praise rendered to him in this great hymn, while the gods of the nations are completely worthless. They are unable to do for their followers all that God can do for his people. Therefore, the nations are called to abandon their false gods and turn to the one true God and Saviour who will one day judge the whole earth (v 33). The gospel of Jesus Christ demands no less!

**Think about how to stand graciously but firmly for the truth that the God of the Bible is the One True God, in today's increasingly pluralistic world!**

[1] Exod 20:3 [2] 2 Cor 4:4, NRSV



**BIBLE IN A YEAR:** Ecclesiastes 4,5; 2 Thessalonians 3

# NO PUNCHES PULLED

**David paints a bleak picture of what the godless are like, but assures us that their wickedness does not go unseen. In contrast, salvation and joy await the believer!**

**PSALM 14**

It is hard to imagine atheists existing in David's day. After all, archaeology has revealed the very religious nature of the peoples of the Ancient Near East. They believed in many gods. David's treatise on the folly of atheism is therefore less to do with philosophical debate about whether the God of Israel exists than with the practical outworking of a refusal to believe in and obey him. Such unbelief results in the moral depravity David records in his psalm. Its message is so fundamental that it is repeated with slight variation in Psalm 53. The apostle Paul reiterates it in Romans 3, but extends it to encompass not only atheists but the whole human race.

David makes clear how devoid of good the godless are. Their wickedness manifests itself in exploitation of the poor (v 6) and persecution of God's people (v 4). How relevant this is today, when Christians are increasingly reviled in the world and the divide between rich and poor gets ever bigger! What the 'fool' of David's day and the God-deniers of our time ignore is the fact that the Lord is looking down upon them (v 2). One day they will be filled with dread (v 5) when he manifests his presence among them.

That occasion will bring salvation for Israel out of Zion and the restoration of the fortunes of God's people (v 7). David thus gives us a vision of the Messiah's coming in splendour. It will be a day of reckoning, when the darkness of foolish unbelief will be exposed in the dazzling light of God's righteousness. First-century Jewish philosopher Philo wrote, 'He who tries to flee from God takes refuge in himself'.[1] That refuge will seem truly paltry on the great day of the Lord!

**Reflect on why it is important that we believe in a God of righteousness and justice in today's corrupt world. Give thanks for his grace, freely offered to repentant sinners.**

1 Philo, *Legum allegoriarum* (Allegorical Interpretation), Book III, 29

**BIBLE IN A YEAR:** Ecclesiastes 6,7; Psalms 95,96

# GOD KNOWS BEST

**'The road to hell is paved with good intentions' may be true, and sometimes our good intentions to do something for God may not be what God intends for us.**

## 1 CHRONICLES 17:1–15

Thankful for all that God has given him, David decides to build a Temple for the Ark in place of the tent he had erected in Jerusalem. Through the prophet Nathan, God effectively tells the king, 'Thanks, but no thanks!' David will not build the Temple, because he had shed much blood in God's sight.[1] However, this is no curt rebuff, for God ultimately shows his approval of the king by promising to build David a house (a dynasty)! Building the Temple is simply not part of his plan for David's life. Two lessons emerge from the passage.

First, we see how utterly generous God is. David seeks to honour God by doing something wonderful for him. God is certainly honoured by David's good intention, but he shows the superabundance of his own generosity by promising David something infinitely more wonderful than David could offer him. Hebrews 6:10 assures us that God 'will not forget your work and the love you have shown him'. He owes us nothing, of course. At the same time, he delights to lavish blessings on us. We can be certain that we can never out-give the Lord!

Second, sometimes, like David, we have something in mind that we want to do for God. Perhaps we long for a certain spiritual gift we believe will help us to serve God better. Or maybe there's a task we feel we can do that will bring him glory. Again, an emotional appeal for workers at a missionary rally might make me feel I should volunteer. What if God says 'no' to our good intentions? Are we prepared, like David, to accept God's better plan and allow his will to supersede ours? The old Christian cliché is nonetheless true: 'My disappointments are his appointments!'

**Speak to God about your disappointments, whatever they may be. Tell him honestly how you feel about them and finish with 'not my will, but yours be done'.[2]**

[1] 1 Chr 22:8 [2] Luke 22:42

 **BIBLE IN A YEAR:** Ecclesiastes 8,9; 1 Timothy 1

# PAST MERCIES, FUTURE HOPE

**When we remember how God faithfully saw us through challenges and trials in the past, it encourages us to entrust our lives to his loving care for the future.**

**1 CHRONICLES 17:16–27**

John Newton, ex-slave-trader turned Anglican priest, often wrote hymns to accompany his sermons. He and fellow hymn-writer, William Cowper, published a three-volume hymnal in 1779, titled *The Olney Hymns*. Their hymns were arranged according to the biblical text that had inspired them. Volume One includes a hymn called 'Faith's Review and Expectation', written to accompany the sermon Newton preached on New Year's Day 1773. The sermon and hymn were based on verses 16 and 17 of today's reading, where King David manifests his amazement at all that God had done for him and was going to do.

Newton encouraged his listeners to follow David's example and consider God's 'past mercies and future hopes' in 'the frame of mind which becomes us when we contemplate what the Lord has done for us'.[1] We know that hymn by another name: 'Amazing Grace'. It has become a firm favourite with Christians all over the world. It even affected the destiny of a nation, after appearing in Harriet Beecher Stowe's book, *Uncle Tom's Cabin*, published in 1852. Sung by the book's black slave hero, Tom, its words express ultimate hope in God in the midst of deepest suffering and injustice. The book laid bare the wickedness of slavery and cried out for its demise in the USA.

When we as Christians are facing trials, it does our hearts good to review how God rescued us from sin through faith in Christ. He is the Son of David, through whom God's promise in today's passage to establish David's house for ever was to be fulfilled. How encouraging it is to remember times when God delivered us 'through many dangers, toils and snares', as Newton's hymn puts it.

**Have you ever tried 'Bible journalling', ie reading Scripture, pen in hand, noting how it speaks to you each day? Why not give it a go!**

1 http://www.johnnewton.org/Groups/252247/The_John_Newton/new_menus/Sermons/Chronicles/Chronicles.aspx

**BIBLE IN A YEAR:** Ecclesiastes 10,11; 1 Timothy 2

# GREAT EXPECTATIONS

**God gives us many opportunities to serve him well, along with the strength to live in obedience to him. He expects us not to squander them.**

## 1 CHRONICLES 22

Only now are we told why God would not allow David to build the Temple – he had 'shed much blood and fought many wars' (v 8). David did not, however, turn away from God, disappointed at what he was not permitted to do. Instead, he poured his energy and devotion into what he *could* do, by gathering many of the materials that his son Solomon would require for constructing God's house in Jerusalem. How true it is that when God closes one door, he opens another. For David, that meant providing the background support his son would need to accomplish his work. In that sense, David was the Temple's co-builder. How much do those on the front line of Christian ministry depend on others who provide them with spiritual and material support, all of us together co-workers with God in the building of his Temple!

Solomon had every reason to succeed. His father did the groundwork necessary for the Temple's construction and the Lord promised him rest from his enemies and peace during his reign for the fulfilment of his assigned task – but he must be 'careful to observe the decrees and laws that the LORD gave to Moses for Israel' (v 13). Ultimately, in spite of his achievements, Solomon failed! The kingdom divided in two because this 'man of peace and rest' (v 9) relaxed his vigilance when it came to the spiritual enemies ranged against him. The foreign gods of his hundreds of wives and concubines led him astray.[1]

The church's history is riddled with examples of Christian men and women whose lives were full of potential to do great things in God's service, but who let their guard down and fell into sin. In this, we need to be much wiser than Solomon!

**Spend time praying for God's servants on the front line, at home and abroad: pastors, preachers, evangelists, missionaries, etc. Consider how you might better encourage and support them.**

[1] 1 Kings 11



**BIBLE IN A YEAR:** Ecclesiastes 12; 1 Timothy 3

# WORD AND SPIRIT

**In your reading of today's passage, and indeed every day, ask for help from the Holy Spirit to understand and appropriate what God wants to say to you.**

**1 CHRONICLES 28**

In today's housing market, many new homes are presented as 'turn-key' properties. Everything is taken care of (furnishings, appliances, etc). You only need to turn the key and move in! Most people, however, like to furnish and decorate their homes themselves – but they still have little say in the actual construction of their place of residence. A fortunate few are able to draw up personalised plans with an architect.

The Jerusalem Temple was not to be built according to David's or Solomon's plans. Just as he had shown Moses the pattern for the tabernacle,[1] so also the Lord revealed to David a detailed blueprint of how the Temple was to be built. We do not know exactly how this happened, but somehow God's Spirit impressed upon David's mind what this magnificent edifice was to look like (vs 12,19). CH Spurgeon's comment is most appropriate: 'If God was to be the Tenant, should it not be built to suit him? And who knows what God requires in a habitation but God himself?'[2]

The same principle applies to the construction of God's spiritual house, built on the foundation of Christ and made up of Christians, its 'living stones'.[3] This house is the new-covenant Temple, where God dwells by his Holy Spirit. About this great edifice, Jesus says 'I will build my church, and the gates of hell shall not prevail against it'.[4] The Bible is the only God-given blueprint for its construction, under the masterful direction of its divine Architect, the Holy Spirit. Word and Spirit together – what a glorious combination ensuring the successful completion of that heaven-designed Temple! Let us be careful to stick to God's blueprint!

**The church is not a building, but the people of which it is formed. It holds firm when its 'living stones' stick together. Pray for Christian unity and harmony.**

[1] Exod 25:8,9 [2] http://thekingdomcollective.com/spurgeon/sermon/2280/
[3] 1 Pet 2:5 [4] Matt 16:18, ESV

**BIBLE IN A YEAR:** Song Of Songs 1,2; Psalms 97,98

# WHO ARE YOUR ROLE MODELS?

**David's generosity towards God is a measure of his heartfelt gratitude for God's generosity towards him. How thankful are you for all that God means to you?**

## 1 CHRONICLES 29:1–20

'Follow my example, as I follow the example of Christ', exhorts the apostle Paul.[1] That might sound arrogant and boastful to the modern ear. However, Paul is simply assuming authority for his God-given message, urging us to be faithful to it as he was. We benefit greatly from good role models, men and women we can look to as examples to be imitated. They put flesh on the bones of theoretical principles. Sadly, in today's world, many follow the lead of celebrity role models whose dissolute lifestyles have little to recommend them. By contrast, in today's chapter we see David as a profoundly positive role model.

David has already contributed much from the national treasury towards the building of God's Temple in Jerusalem. Now, as his life draws to an end, he digs deep into his own pocket in favour of this great God-honouring construction project. His example is a challenge for his officials to consider and a model for them to imitate. They contribute massively, in a way that recalls the tabernacle's construction in Moses' time.[2] Their generosity fills David's and his people's hearts with joy, leading them to praise and worship God.

How we use our material wealth can be a thorny issue for Christians. Some apply very strictly the old-covenant principle of tithing. Others believe that tithing is just a start and must be augmented by the outpouring of a grateful heart in financial sacrifices and offerings. Whatever we give, it must be done joyfully[3] and, although we must not trumpet our righteousness,[4] it nevertheless blesses us to learn of the sacrificial giving of others whose liberality encourages ours. God is exalted in the generous giving of his people!

**'God loves a cheerful giver.'[5] Do you give to God's work out of a sense of duty or with a thankful heart? Reflect a moment on this.**

[1] 1 Cor 11:1 [2] Exod 35:4 – 36:7 [3] 2 Cor 9:7 [4] Matt 6:1–4 [5] 2 Cor 9:7

 **BIBLE IN A YEAR:** Song Of Songs 3,4; 1 Timothy 4

# GREAT DAVID'S GREATER SON

**God's promises to David were fulfilled in David's heavenly Descendant, Jesus Christ. David's rule is a pale reflection of what Christ's reign will look like.**

**1 CHRONICLES 29:21–30**

David's reign is ending. He will share the throne as co-regent with Solomon for a short time, before dying at a good old age. The warrior-king will be succeeded by the prince of peace. There, in this royal tandem, we have an image of the Son of David to come – King Jesus, the supreme Warrior-King[1] and Prince of Peace.[2] Today's passage gives us two interesting details. First, Solomon was acknowledged as king twice (v 22). Second, the throne he occupied is called the Lord's (v 23).

David's son, Adonijah, had tried to make himself king of Israel.[3] He was not God's choice: Solomon was. So David checkmated Adonijah by anointing Solomon in a rather humble ceremony stripped of the usual coronation trappings.[4] Solomon's second glorious enthronement is the exact opposite. Similarly, great David's greater Son, Jesus, was recognised as King the first time by foreign astrologers in the humblest of settings.[5] His earthly existence was far from royal – but he will return a second time, to be proclaimed in glory, and then all the nations will acknowledge him.[6]

Solomon was king only under God's authority and sat on 'the throne of the LORD' (v 23) only because God had set it up and promised to establish it for ever. That promise was to be fulfilled through a descendant of David's royal line, as explained to his mother Mary.[7] As Christians, we wait in eager anticipation for the coming of our King, when at last his usurper, 'the god of this world',[8] will be cast aside and Christ's universal authority acknowledged. As we say 'goodbye' to David, we longingly turn to his greater Son, praying, 'Maranatha! Come, Lord!'

**George Whitefield, the great 18th-century English evangelist, said, 'I am daily waiting for the coming of the Son of God'. How much do you long for Christ's return?**

**1** Rev 19:11–16 **2** Isa 9:6 **3** 1 Kings 1:1–27 **4** 1 Kings 1:38,39 **5** Matt 2:1–12 **6** Matt 25:31–33; Phil 2:9–11 **7** Luke 1:31–33 **8** 2 Cor 4:4, NRSV

**BIBLE IN A YEAR:** Song Of Songs 5,6; 1 Timothy 5

# INTEGRITY

**We cannot enter God's presence just any old how. Our hearts and lives must be in tune with God for our worship to be acceptable to him.**

## PSALM 15

David may have composed this psalm to celebrate the Ark of the Covenant being brought to Jerusalem. We cannot be sure of this, but the words certainly suit that occasion. They describe the character of the person the Lord welcomes to worship at his tabernacle. Such a person was David himself. In spite of his failings as recorded in Scripture, God called him 'a man after my own heart'.[1] What an encouragement it is to remember that God loves and uses fallen people like David and us to fulfil his purposes!

However, Psalm 15 allows us to make no excuses for our failures. Its portrayal of the true worshipper's character can be summed up in one word: *integrity* – 'the quality of being honest and having strong moral principles that you refuse to change'.[2] That quality is greatly missing in today's world. Dishonourable dealings within the finance industry triggered the 2007 economic crisis. That it should happen 'in the world' is bad enough, but frequent moral and financial scandals within the church remind Christians that, for every finger we point at another, three are pointing back at us. And remember, the church is not just its leaders, but all who are part of it! How do we fare individually in the integrity stakes? How much of Psalm 15 is true of you and me?

Of course, in the new-covenant age, we enter God's presence by grace through faith in Christ, not by our works, but that grace is not cheap! It cost God dearly. Let us not forget: 'We must all appear before the judgement seat of Christ, so that each of us may receive what is due to us for the things done while in the body, whether good or bad'.[3]

**The world loves it when church leaders fall into scandal. Today, pray for the protection, blessing and holiness of those in positions of Christian leadership over us.**

[1] Acts 13:22 [2] http://dictionary.cambridge.org/dictionary/english/integrity
[3] 2 Cor 5:10



**BIBLE IN A YEAR:** Song Of Songs 7,8; Psalms 99–101

# DESERT SPIRITUALITY

**CLAIRE DALPRA**

Some years ago, life threw me a curve ball. Suddenly, my life was on a different trajectory – one that I never anticipated. Feelings of disappointment, grief and, at times, anger bubbled away beneath the surface of my life. I didn't lose my Christian faith but something about my faith did change. I couldn't sing upbeat choruses or rousing hymns in the same way. I found it more difficult to listen to sermons. I wasn't cynical or disbelieving; it just all seemed a bit distant. Until that point, I hadn't realised how unconsciously I had lived with the naïve assumption that being a Christian equalled a happy, trouble-free life.

I mention my experience because I suspect quite a few of us go through such times, or know of others who do. One of my challenges was knowing to whom I could talk about it – I was very aware that sharing my woes with someone was a bit of a mood-killer. Other frustrations were Christian friends who either turned defensive or were annoyingly quick to impose on me their well-meaning solutions.

Help came to me from a place I never expected. I work for an organisation called Church Army. One of the quirks of this wonderful mission community is the way it embraces the variety of church traditions within the Anglican church. When my curve ball hit, I found myself enveloped by a small, slightly oddball, group of Church Army Evangelists who were exploring a strand of Christian spirituality called the apophatic tradition.

Apophatic prayer is a form of contemplative prayer without words; it is prayer practised silently, acknowledging the poverty of our language – and to some extent our imagination – in understanding and expressing who God is. Yet, the apophatic tradition does not abandon all use of imagery. Deserts, mountains and other threatening places are used as ways to describe and explore the internal landscape of the soul when you feel lost and you feel that you've lost God.

### WISDOM ABOUT FAITH AND SUFFERING

The search for the mysterious and elusive presence of God by his people is a familiar theme, weaving its way through the Old

Testament writings. The book of Job offers a unique contribution to this; it is an almost mythical story set in an unspecified period of history, structured for the most part as poetry and written in an unusual kind of Hebrew. Job, a prosperous man and faithful servant of God, loses everything, suffers greatly and, along with four not-very-helpful-friends, tries to understand why.

Unlike the rest of the wisdom literature of the Old Testament, the book of Job does not follow the usual argument that righteousness is rewarded and wickedness is punished. It is provocative. Job is an innocent sufferer - more commonly found in the psalmic tradition - 'planted' into the wisdom literature to delve deeper into faith and suffering where there are no easy answers.[1] Most scholars agree that the story of Job teaches us that personal suffering is not deserved but neither is it God's fault. At risk of oversimplifying what is reassuringly rich in complexity, we conclude that God is the one who stands with us in our suffering when all others have deserted us.

After the whirlwind of God's appearance into the story and the glimpse into his divine power and majesty, Job replies 'Surely I spoke of things I did not understand, things too wonderful for me to know' (42:3). This verse is one of many that inspires the apophatic tradition. Along with Moses' interaction with God on Mount Sinai, where God is shrouded in cloud or darkness, seen only in part, theologians of the early church such as Gregory of Nyssa argued that God was incomprehensible, obscure and found 'there where the understanding does not reach'.[2]

#### TREASURES OF THE DESERT TRADITION

I am indebted to a book that has been my teacher: *The Solace of Fierce Landscapes* by Belden C Lane, an American professor of theology at Saint Louis University. This wonderfully informative yet evocative book introduces the reader to leading figures such as 6th-century Pseudo Dionysius the Areopagite, who first used the term apophatic (along with the term 'kataphatic'[3]) to describe this kind of prayer.

1 David JA Clines, *Word Biblical Commentary*, Volume 18a Job 21–37, 2006, Thomas Nelson, p524 2 Belden C Lane, *The Solace of Fierce Landscapes: Exploring Desert and Mountain Spirituality*, Oxford University Press, 1988 3 The kataphatic tradition uses image, metaphor and imagination in its contemplation of God

Julian of Norwich, a 14th-century ascetic nun, also explored this idea of vulnerability following her mystical experience during an illness. She suggested that, like a hazelnut, we are very small. We could have fallen into nothingness, yet we exist only because we are loved by God.[4] The loss of control that comes with abandoning language in prayer helps us become aware of our smallness, knowing that God the Trinity loves us deeply in our helplessness.

The anonymous author of *The Cloud of Unknowing* was drawn by the image of Sinai and wrote that a cloud always separates the believer from God. Accepting the cloud is the key, and the way to accept the cloud is to empty yourself through a self-forgetfulness that allows 'the deeper, truer self' to enter prayer 'in darkness and trust'.[5] In a similar way, Meister Eckhart, a 14th-century German monk, wrote that we must strip away everything that would distract us in prayer, to enter a nothingness that goes deep in contemplation of the Godhead.

**WHAT DOES DESERT SPIRITUALITY TEACH US?**

The desert tradition, Lane writes, identifies two apparently contradictory disciplines: attentiveness and indifference. Attentiveness in the desert is about monitoring your levels of fatigue or dehydration and watching the weather for the slightest change that indicates the onslaught of a sandstorm. For those in a *spiritual* desert, attentiveness is about learning to be quiet, being fully present to one's self and to others, watching for the subtle presence of God in our lives.

Indifference arises from the harshness of the physical desert environment, so unyielding to human presence. In the *spiritual* desert, indifference isn't the sort of apathy that throws out a sulky 'I don't care' to the world. Instead, it's to do with quieting the ego with all its personal desires and becoming 'equally indifferent to the praise or the blame of the world'. It is about cultivating disinterestedness in the success and attention that our egos so often crave.[6] Lane summarises the relationship of these two desert disciplines as

**4** Julian of Norwich, *Revelations of Divine Love*, Penguin, 1966, p68 **5** Lane, p73 **6** Lane, p193

'being attentive to what matters and indifferent to what doesn't matter'.[7]

Perhaps the best known author in this tradition is John of the Cross. His writings are a bewildering mix of severity and gentleness, exploring that deep mysterious love that is born in the experience of loss. Drawing on Song of Songs, the Psalms and Jesus' teaching, John argued that we can only be free to love God if we embrace our weakness. We go 'into the darkness of the night with heart ache kindled into love'.[8] This is what the desert experience does to us; it intensifies our longing for the one who seems so elusive.

### THE PRACTICALITIES OF WORDLESS PRAYER

Explaining the practice of 'wordless prayer' to other Christians often results in them regarding me as if I were slightly unhinged. 'But what do you actually do in prayer?' they ask. I ought to add that I am no expert; like with any spiritual practice, I have seasons when I'm disciplined and seasons when I lapse. I know it's not for everyone, but it might just offer a glimmer of hope to anyone struggling with a curve ball.

Even now, I hesitate to lay out a how-to guide; it is the sort of thing you discover by yourself or with fellow companions (like my Church Army group). As much as I'd like to adopt a meditative lotus position, I'm not as supple as I used to be so I just opt for a relaxed sitting position. Lighting a candle helps too; I love Lauren Winner's reflections on candle-lighting as a spiritual practice and the thought that lighting a candle is a sign of trying to pay attention.[9]

Then I set my timer for 20 minutes, concentrate on my breathing and descend into stillness, watching and waiting. I find a peace that doesn't have all the answers but feels alive and close to God in the mystery of so much that is unknown. The silence that used to be unsettling is now a silence that carries with it the power to connect and heal and, in the words of May Sarton, 'I am lavish with riches made from loss'.[10]

---

[7] Lane, p188 [8] St John of the Cross, *The Dark Night of the Soul*, Hodder Christian Classics, 1988, p1 [9] Lauren Winner, *Mudhouse Sabbath*, Paraclete Press, 2003, p112
[10] May Sarton, *A Durable Fire*, from the poem 'The Contemplation of Wisdom', Open Road Media, 2014

# MATTHEW 21:28 – 22:46

## THE FINAL DEBATES

The drama that Jesus had outlined to his disciples a few days earlier[1] enters a new act, moving inexorably towards its seemingly inevitable conclusion. The scene has shifted from Galilee and the Jordan area, to Jerusalem, the seat of political and religious power. Jesus' dramatic Palm Sunday entry, disrupting the commercial enterprise of the Temple, has stirred the city. The Pharisees, the Sadducees and the Herodians are forced to face this challenge, starting by questioning the basis of Jesus' authority. This week we consider his response. On the one hand, he answers the questions posed to him; on the other hand, he initiates debate. Primarily he is challenging these groups of Jewish leaders to be the true guides of the people of God.

The parables, allegories and images that Jesus uses in these chapters work in a variety of ways. First, they relate to the environment and customs his audience knows - and that raises a problem for us. Few of us have planted a vineyard. Weddings are celebrated differently in different cultures and marriage laws differ. We are not subject to an occupying power. So, second, we as readers need to delve into the detail, identify the single point that Jesus is making and relate it to who we are and the communities in which we live. Often Jesus helps us to sharpen our focus by his perceptive commentary, but we need to constantly be aware of the application here and now.

By the end of the week we reach the end of the formal disputing. The Pharisees, Sadducees and Herodians are confused, caught in a quandary and dare not renew the challenge - at least not in this form. They are forced to regroup,[2] coming to the conclusion that the occupying Roman authorities must be involved. Jesus' response is to turn to the crowds, the common people and his disciples.

***Brian Radcliffe***

[1] Matt 20:17–19 [2] Matt 26:3–5

# YOUR STARTER FOR 10

**Imagine yourself in the *Mastermind* chair with God as the question master. Put on one side the questions and requests you have for him and prepare to listen.**

## MATTHEW 21:28–32

Have you ever come in halfway through a conversation and tried to work out what's going on? We're in that position now. Jesus has previously posed a question to the chief priests and elders about attitudes to John the Baptist's authority to baptise.[1] The common people had responded to John, accepting him as God's messenger; the religious authorities (who should have known better) rejected him. So Jesus presses the point, saying: 'Let's put it another way: what do you think about this example?' and leads them step by step through a story about saying and doing.

It's easy to say we'll do something when it's requested of us. Often we fully intend to do so, but occasionally we forget. At other times we say we'll do what was requested but in reality have no intention of doing so. We're simply trying to get someone off our back. On the other hand, we sometimes say that we're not able to meet a request but it niggles away at us until we're forced to go and do it, willingly or unwillingly. So, Jesus concludes, even the worst in society (the ubiquitous tax collectors and shameful prostitutes) responded to John's niggling and entered the kingdom of God, whereas God's yes-men, the religious leaders, by their choice are left outside. In saying this, Jesus has clearly demonstrated his right to distinguish between those who choose the righteous way and those who do not. Their question about spiritual authority has been answered in no uncertain terms.

In Jesus' story there are two things for us to receive: first, that doing is what actually matters, actions really do speak louder than words, as in the parable of the fruit of the good tree,[2] and, second, that if the cap fits we must wear it. Clearly the chief priests and elders found this impossible.

**What is niggling away at you? Is now the time to get up and do it?**

[1] Matt 21:24,25a [2] Matt 7:15–20

**BIBLE IN A YEAR:** Isaiah 1,2; 1 Timothy 6

# THE PENNY DROPS

**Invite God to come into this time with patience, as you acknowledge how slow you can be to understand and respond to his words.**

## MATTHEW 21:33–46

Some people take a long time to catch on. They need a further prompt. So Jesus tells another parable, drawing the Pharisees and elders towards an unavoidable conclusion. The vineyard was both an agricultural reality and a profound symbol for his listeners. As scholars, they would recognise the references to Isaiah 5:1–7 (planting new vines, the construction of a winepress and a watchtower) and the spelling out of the symbol in verse 7a: 'The vineyard of the LORD Almighty is the house of Israel' (TNIV). One by one, the truth would dawn on these leaders – that he was talking about them. They were the unreliable, the self-serving, the aggressive tenants.

Sometimes, when reading the Bible or listening to a sermon, I recognise others in the message. At my more perceptive, I admit that I myself am also in there. In my best moments I'm drawn to confession and repentance. Such was the initial response Jesus hoped for from his audience, but he also wanted to lay before them a scenario for the days to follow. The murder of the son is part of the logical growth in violence throughout the story. Can he now get his audience to see that he is that son?

The Pharisees and elders deliver their self-righteous verdict as the tenants get their just desserts. Then they are surprised to find themselves in the dock: 'Therefore I tell you that the kingdom of God will be taken away from *you* and given to a people who will produce its fruit' (v 43, italics added). *Touché*, as the French say. There is still a chance for them, as there was for the tenants at any point in the story, to give the owner his due. They recognise their role in the story. Their reaction? Kill the messenger!

**Retell the parable to yourself. Bring to mind those who in the past brought God's message to you. Send a letter, an email, a phone message to thank them.**



**BIBLE IN A YEAR:** Isaiah 3–5; 2 Timothy 1

# GOOD ENOUGH FOR CHURCH?

**Bring to mind the members of your church and think of their similarities and differences in terms of age, gender, ethnic origin and social class.**

**MATTHEW 22:1–14**

The background changes from a vineyard to a wedding reception, from a farmer to a king, but the result is just the same – at least for the servants who are tasked with delivering the invitations. They are met with refusals; they are ignored, seized, beaten up and killed. In the end, the king extends an open invitation to the event, welcoming 'the bad as well as the good' (v 10).

When I was young there were accepted ground rules for attending church. I was to wear school uniform, sit quietly and listen; above all to be good, regardless of how boring the service was and how little relevance the worship style and sermon had to the vibrant cultural explosion of the mid-1960s on Merseyside. Although mine was an evangelical church, there was little connection with the down-and-dirty side of the community. Not surprisingly, few from there had the courage to enter the forbidding doors.

Social theologians suggest that there are two types of churches. First, there are those described as a bounded set – a closed membership that shares certain privileges. To enter the membership it is necessary to conform to statements of faith, meet attendance expectations and take part in training and incorporating rituals. Second, there are those churches that are described as a centred set, where members are committed to worshipping God at the centre but may well be doing so with differing measures of faith and doubt. Here there's a very faint boundary indeed: everyone is invited as long as their intention (their wedding clothes) is to press on to discover more about God.[1] That sounds very much like the king's final invitation.

**Make contact with someone in your church family who is totally unlike you. This might be by phone, email, letter or a spontaneous visit. Enjoy their company.**

1 Phil 3:14

# GIVE ME A STRAIGHT ANSWER

**Bring to mind a piece of dense woodland that you are familiar with. Imagine trying to find a pathway through it. Invite God to accompany you.**

## MATTHEW 22:15–22

In the English language there are two types of question. Open questions encourage an answer that is developed, giving options and inviting a continuing debate. Closed questions, like the one set before Jesus, demand a yes or a no. So, the unholy alliance of Pharisees and Herodians sets Jesus a trap. If his answer is yes, then the Herodians are pleased as it justifies their policy of collaboration with the Romans, but the Pharisees are given reason to incite the crowd (which doesn't like Roman oppression) against Jesus. If his answer is no, then the Pharisees identify Jesus as a political rebel and the Herodians can charge him with sedition.

Closed questions see the world as black and white. It makes life simpler. Yet reality is rarely like this. Living by faith is about hope rather than certainty, about what we can't see rather than what is always clear and obvious.[1] Living by faith is sometimes about acknowledging that there is more than one side to an issue, just as Jesus does here. In our contemporary world that might include such issues as politics, wealth and medical ethics. Maybe living by faith is one long open question, in which doubt and uncertainty are constant companions – along with belief and assurance. This is how it was for the disciple Thomas and the father of the child healed by Jesus.[2]

Jesus' open response to the closed question hinges on the phrase 'give back' in verse 21. Tax is payment for the benefits we receive from a structured society. Praise, worship and obedience are what we give back to God for who he is and for what he has done and continues to do for us. There is no contradiction. We are citizens of two kingdoms.

**Take a copy of today's news and note each story that is hard to reconcile with your Christian faith. Ask God for wisdom in understanding the issues.**

1 Heb 11:1 2 John 20:24–29; Mark 9:23,24

 **BIBLE IN A YEAR:** Isaiah 8,9; Psalm 102

# TAKE IT TO THE LIMIT

**Recall an incident where your Christian faith was mocked. How did it feel? What were your reactions?**

**MATTHEW 22:23–33**

I enjoy a good puzzle, a sudoku or a crossword, particularly when on holiday. So the Sadducees, the priestly aristocracy, come to Jesus with a brainteaser. They take a simple situation, the life of a widow, and push it to its limit, what we term 'reductio ad absurdum'. Whose wife will she be at the resurrection? The question is absurd, even more so since the Sadducees don't believe in the resurrection anyway. To them, the soul dies along with the body. So what's going on? I suggest that rather than initiating a genuine theological discussion it appears that the Sadducees simply want to make Jesus look foolish.

I find it hard to cope with being made to look a fool. It undermines my self-confidence, questioning my intellect, my ability, my knowledge, my common sense, my maturity. It has happened within church – a biting comment in a house study group, questioning of my interpretation of a Bible passage, criticism of my pastoral sensitivity – but it is more often a tactic used by those who have no time for my faith (or any faith at all). Ridicule and undermining are used to bolster their view of the world. I'm reduced to biting my tongue at best, but can be tempted to bite back defensively with words I later regret.

Jesus' response is to turn to Scripture. It's objective. This is what it says. To the Sadducees, versed in the Torah, the quotation cannot be denied. They have to consider the passage and are reduced to silence (v 34). The reaction of the crowd (v 33) illustrates that Jesus is a teacher who commands respect.

**Scripture is our bedrock, even when others don't accept its value. Commit yourself to study and to memorising some key passages.**

# IN A NUTSHELL

**What are your priorities for today? Do you have plans already made, or are you open to change? Invite God into your schedule.**

## MATTHEW 22:34–46

We expect the final question posed to Jesus to be the most explosive, the one that demolishes his claim to who he is. The Pharisees even bring out their key player, their top expert, to challenge him. Yet in the end this is no harsh test for Jesus. His answer is orthodox: the greatest commandment is that given in Deuteronomy 6:5 – to love God with your whole being. These words were repeated daily by Jewish people as part of the Shema prayer. God must come first. What Jesus does that is interesting is that he immediately links this to human behaviour. 'Love your neighbour as yourself'[1] completes the dual focus of a life of faith. Everything is summed up by these two commands.

Augustine's words 'Love God and do as you please' works for me as a philosophy for life. Similarly, posing the question 'What would Jesus do?' helps when I'm faced with a quandary. If I could see the world through God's eyes, if Jesus were to step into my situations, then I would know how to follow. As it is, it is only through offering the whole of my being to him – my emotions, my spirit, my intellect – that I can begin to glimpse what life would be like with him in charge. So to live with the nuts and bolts of acting lovingly towards those I meet and those whose lives I affect in a wider context must start with knowing God himself and his revelation to me in Jesus.

Finally, Jesus poses his own question: 'What do you think about the Messiah?' (v 42). It is now the Pharisees who beat the retreat. Without a word being said, it is clear that here is someone who offers them the biggest challenge to their authority that they have ever faced.

**Look again at today's schedule. What would a loving God do in the hours that remain of today? Do you need to make any changes?**

[1] Lev 19:18

# I'M IN A GOOD PLACE

**Name three aspects of your life that give you pleasure right now. Thank God for each of them.**

**PSALM 16**

Depression is an illness that hangs over society, including many in church. Cognitive behaviour therapy (CBT) is a strategy that helps to manage depression partly by focusing on the good things in life. Psalm 16 is a CBT psalm. It's full of pleasure, security, joy and hope for the future. 'The boundary lines [of life] have fallen for me in pleasant places' (v 6a). The psalm assures us that there's a time and a place to be contented rather than worried. We have no need to feel guilty about it. We have no need to hide it. We simply should give God his due.

How can we arrive in such a place of contentment? The psalm says it comes totally from reliance on God (v 2). Other potential sources (money, sex and power come to mind for a start) are not worth the effort (v 4). Even the company we keep can contribute to our pleasure if it is also God-driven. And it's not just for now. Since our future is secure (vs 9,10) we can rest, relax and enjoy life.

Today is God's day, traditionally set aside by Christians for worship, family and relaxation. Psalm 16 paints a picture of how it can feel. If it doesn't, then maybe we need to look at how we're spending our time. Do we sometimes need to set our boundary lines a little more clearly? Can work, worries and the expectations of others not remain beyond the boundary for today? It's not always an easy task, as most of society sees Sunday as little different to any other day. However, with God in control there's enough time for these things tomorrow, when our physical, spiritual and emotional batteries are fully recharged and we're in a positive frame of mind.

**Think of every issue that invades your peace and contentment. Imagine driving them, like a flock of sheep or a herd of cows, into a fenced-off field, for tomorrow.**

**BIBLE IN A YEAR:** Isaiah 15,16; Psalm 103

# AMOS

## LIFESTYLE AND WORSHIP

Lions and earthquakes, crimes and cows, repulsive worship and false security: just some of the themes of this book. At first glance it is all doom and gloom, but if we dig beneath the surface we can find evidence of God's incredible love. Amos is an ordinary farmer from Judah, who obeys God's call to warn the northern kingdom of Israel of coming judgement unless they undergo a radical change of heart. He does this through setting a trap, debating with his hearers, relaying visions and using powerful rhetoric.

If we think this doesn't apply to us, we should think again. We need to examine our own lives: the temptation to assimilate to the attitudes of the world around us; the tendency to think that as long as our worship songs move us, God will be pleased; the temptation to excesses, when so many live in poverty. If we are leaders in the church, are we ordinary enough to empathise with those we lead? Are we compassionate, prayerful, courageous?

For Israel, at that time in their history, when many felt secure and prosperous and were ignoring God's covenant requirements, they had to learn that God's presence was to be reckoned with. Sin does not have the last word, however, and Amos gives us hints of the love of God that could not leave his people in their desperate state. If judgement were the only way to get their attention, so be it. He still shouts through our pain! He has not given up on his people: for those who own him as Lord and Saviour, his commitment to love leads to forgiveness and restoration. But his choice of us carries with it great responsibility – so, how are we doing?

***Vivien Whitfield***

### FOR FURTHER READING

E Achtemeier, *Minor Prophets* 1, Hendrickson, 1996

DA Hubbard, *Joel and Amos*, IVP, 1989

Karl Möller, *Reading Amos as a Book*, Grove booklet, B74, 2014. This is an excellent overview of the message of Amos, read as a whole, with helpful questions for reflection.

# THE ROARING LION

**Thank God for his great mercy towards you – and remember what it cost him.**

**AMOS 1:1–10**

Lions at the zoo in my childhood never appeared fierce – and they were fed butcher's meat. How very different from hungry lions in the wild; how terrifying for their prey to hear the roar, to sense the pounce of rippling muscles and to feel the tearing claws! This is how Amos pictures God (v 2). Can he really be like that?

Amos' first speeches would have had Israel chortling with glee. These neighbouring nations had done terrible things; it was time they felt God's fiery anger.[1] Damascus had practised excessive cruelty in war. The Philistines had engaged in a lucrative slave-trading business, the helpless being abused in the pursuit of material wealth. Tyre was also involved in slave trading, but its crime was even worse because it acted in breach of a 'treaty of brotherhood' (v 9). The punishments would fit the crimes, leaving the perpetrators vulnerable themselves. None of these nations had received any special revelation of God or his law, so idolatry is not mentioned: they were under judgement for their inhumanity. Accountability to God has always been proportionate to the knowledge of his will granted to a people. As we shall see, Israel itself was judged much more harshly, because it had been given God's law. From everyone to whom much is given, much will be required.[2]

Similar horrendous cruelty goes on in many parts of the world today. In our desire to share God's love, it is easy to forget how angry he is in the face of such behaviour. Yes, God will one day judge evil as a roaring lion tears its prey, but the Lion of Judah was also the Lamb who was slain.[3] At the cross, where wrath and mercy meet, there is opportunity for even the worst perpetrator to repent and find forgiveness.

**When you hear of terrorist atrocities, how do you pray?**

---

**1** The fire of judgement appears in each section of this reading (vs 4,7,10)
**2** Luke 12:48 **3** Rev 5:5–10

# THE NOOSE TIGHTENS

**'You desire truth in the inward being; therefore teach me wisdom in my secret heart.'[1]**

## AMOS 1:11 – 2:5

One child hurts another. Justice is required. Punishment of the offender is delighted in: 'Serves him right!' Israel would probably have chortled over the punishment of Edom, Ammon and Moab. These nations were cousins to Israel – and Judah was even more a part of the family; between Israel and Judah there had existed a precarious relationship for hundreds of years. Did Israel feel smug? The people believed they were God's favourites. Let the others be punished for what they had done to Israel!

Edom (Esau) was Israel's (Jacob's) twin,[2] but Edom continually harassed his brother Israel, with implacable hatred. Ammon's territory was cramped; in its restless pursuit of land it practised unspeakable atrocities against women (a feature of ancient warfare,[3] also practised against Jews by Hitler's troops in the second world war). Moab violated the mores of the ancient world.[4] God's anger against Judah (Amos' homeland) was not for inhumanity, as it was for the other peoples: Judah's crime was rejecting God's law (and therefore God himself) and assimilation of neighbouring idolatrous practices ('lies', 2:4, note in NIV). Judah's breach of covenant with God was far worse than those of Tyre and Edom with a brother nation. Judah had acted as heathen, so would now be treated as such, although in practice the judgement was averted for 135 years.

We, who have a fuller revelation of God in Jesus Christ and his written Word, have a huge responsibility to be faithful to him. The temptation to assimilate the practices and attitudes of the world around us is very strong. In many cases we perhaps don't even realise what is happening, but when anything becomes more important to us than God, we are being led astray. May we not fall into temptation.

**Lord, forgive us that so often we fail to keep our cutting edge as your disciples, allowing the world around us to pull us away from your priorities.**

1 Ps 51:6, NRSV 2 Gen 25:21–26 3 2 Kings 8:12,15; Hos 13:16; Achtemeier, p182 4 Cf 2 Kings 9:34

 **BIBLE IN A YEAR:** Isaiah 21,22; Titus 2

# WEATHER BOMB!

**'All have sinned and fall short of the glory of God.'[1]**

**AMOS 2:6–16**

A new term has appeared in colloquial English: 'weather bomb'. Its meteorological definition is 'explosive cyclogenesis' and it describes a superstorm that hits with ferocious intensity, causing huge damage. I rather suspect that would be how it felt for Israel when Amos suddenly turned on them with his bombshell. Yes, Israel too was included in God's judgement! Indeed, far more space is devoted to Israel's wrongdoing than to that of any of its neighbours. Israel's crimes were against the poor, stripping them of human dignity (vs 6,7). They were guilty of rape and carousing within the very house of God, using the proceeds of fines for drink instead of for restitution (vs 7,8), forcing those who attempted to be faithful into going against their conscience and silencing the prophets (vs 11,12).[2]

We can almost feel God's pain as Amos reminds Israel of his goodness to them in the past (vs 9–11): 'I brought you up … and led you …'.[3] The inevitable punishment would come (vs 13–16). God in his love will not leave his people to continue sinning. How could he? If they will not listen to the prophets he sends, they have to learn the hard way.

The message of Amos is very sombre, but we have to remember that it was because of his love that God brought judgement on his people. As we shall see, they more than deserved it – and we can no doubt think of plenty of others who deserve God's judgement today. Of course, we do, too! The wonderful truth, however, is that in Jesus God himself took the punishment for the sin of the world. As we read about injustice, violence and horror in our world today, pray that the gospel will change lives. Then go to work towards making it happen!

**What can you do to further the gospel message and make a difference in your own environment?**

[1] Rom 3:23 [2] For Nazirites see Judg 13:5,7 [3] Hosea portrays this even more strongly (Hos 11:1–4,8)

**BIBLE IN A YEAR:** Isaiah 23,24; Titus 3

# CAUSE AND EFFECT

**God has chosen you in Christ to be his child. Spend some time praising him and thanking him.**

## AMOS 3

A small child runs into a busy road and is narrowly missed by a car. Mum is ferocious in her anger and metes out punishment. Why? Because of the special relationship she has with her child. Similarly, Israel had been hugely privileged to be chosen by God, out of all humanity, to be his instrument for saving the rest of the world. He had lavished his love on the people, saved them from slavery in Egypt and made a covenant agreement with them. They were his children in a special way. So when they repudiated the covenant, risking losing their relationship with God, he had to do something drastic. God 'shouts in our pains' today, too.[1] Allowing us to go through very hard times can sometimes be his way of drawing us back to himself.

The lion has roared (v 8). In answer to Israel's unheard protests, Amos argues from an observed result to an assumed cause. If the result is calamity, the cause has to be God's doing – 'When disaster comes to a city, has not the LORD caused it?' (v 6b) – and Amos has no choice but to announce it (v 8b).[2] Sending Amos was actually part of God's incredible mercy, giving time for repentance, for God does not desire the death of the wicked.[3]

Israel is judged for failing to meet the responsibilities of its election; a sobering thought for God's people today, who have been chosen to be his 'holy nation' to declare his saving acts to the world.[4] His choice of us carries with it responsibility. We are chosen not simply for the privilege of knowing God, the joy of forgiveness and the certainty of eternal life, but also – and inextricably – to serve God's purpose of bringing salvation to his beloved world.[5]

**Ponder Achtemeier's assertion: 'The God of the Bible is a terrifying foe of those who would make him less than Lord over every life and every thing.'[6]**

1 CS Lewis, *The Problem of Pain*, Collins, 1940/1977, p81 2 Hubbard, p157
3 Ezek 18:32 4 1 Pet 2:9,10 5 Achtemeier, p190 6 Achtemeier, p192



**BIBLE IN A YEAR:** Isaiah 25,26; Psalm 104

# PREPARE TO MEET YOUR GOD!

**'Christ died for the ungodly'[1] – even terrorists! Lord, help me to comprehend something of the depth of your love.**

**AMOS 4**

Wealthy women: voluptuous symbols of dissoluteness funded by corrupt oppression of the poor. Amos likens them to well-fed cows of Bashan (a region known for its lush pastures) - but they would be dragged away with hooks, like so much meat.[2]

They were devotedly worshipping at the local shrines and bringing regular (and expensive!) sacrifices and offerings - lots of them (vs 4,5). Their lifestyle did not match up, however, and their elaborate worship rituals were a mere empty show. How could they continue to live when they were profaning God's holy name by their actions and attitudes? The underlying motive for their lavish offerings was to gain status in the community, demonstrating their wealth. Before we condemn them, though, we need to see into our own hearts. Jesus warned against those who made a show of their piety.[3] And not far back in the history of many of us some churchgoers had identical attitudes. In Regency Britain there was a vast gulf between the landed gentry and the poor. Even in the mid twentieth century, the maids knew their place; rich churchgoers could reserve the best pews and woe betide anyone else who tried sitting in them! Substantial giving by Christians was publicly trumpeted. Is there anything like that still lurking in your own church today?

God had repeatedly tried to warn Israel, through the hardships it faced (vs 6–11) - seen as covenant curses.[4] Amos interprets them 'not as a promise of future judgement but as a lens through which to look at past judgement, a lens that focuses not just on the wrath of a betrayed Sovereign but on the grace of One who yearns for restored fellowship with his wayward people.'[5] As I write, London has just suffered a horrific terrorist attack and Archbishop Justin Welby has highlighted the caring medical attention shown to the undeserving attacker. Does that help us to understand God's love for sinners?

**Lord, forgive me – and thank you!**

**1** Rom 5:6 **2** Cf Achtemeier, p197 **3** Matt 6:1–6; see also Luke 21:1–4; James 2:1–7 **4** Deut 28:15–46 **5** Hubbard, p170

**BIBLE IN A YEAR:** Isaiah 27,28; Philemon 1

# LIFE OR DEATH

**Death is part of life; what matters is what precedes it. Lord, I want my life to count; I want to give myself to your service.**

## AMOS 5:1–17

Last winter I seemed to go to a record number of funerals, all different. At some of them, bright colours were worn, in celebration of a life; at others, the mourners wore dark clothing to express their grief and their loss. Amos here speaks a funerary lament which begins and ends with wailing over the dead. The chief mourner is God, who grieves over his unrepentant people and still beseeches them to change their ways (vs 4,6,14,15).

Righteousness was 'a relational term, standing for the fulfilment of the demands of a relationship'.[1] Israel had always been required by God to show mercy to the poor and helpless.[2] That was the requirement of the nation's relationship with people. Instead of this, however, the situation in Israel, as described by Amos, was rife with injustice, corruption and the suppression of those who tried to be just (vs 10,13). Bethel, Gilgal and Beersheba were shrines where Israel had long worshipped, but its upper classes loved themselves rather than God;[3] Amos calls them back to true worship of the Creator God (v 8), worship that will issue in justice and compassion. He calls them to life, real life; not the superficial self-satisfaction of selfishness and greed, but the joyous contentment of those who know God and who pour themselves out for others.

So the funeral draws nearer, but even in its inevitability there is a glimmer of hope that perhaps, just perhaps, Israel might heed the warning (v 15). It may be that someone you know has rebelled against God all their life; there may seem to be little time left for them to change their ways; but keep hoping, keep praying, keep reminding them of their need to 'Seek the LORD and live' (v 6).

**Lord, sometimes change of heart seems impossible, whether in public figures or in people I know personally. May there be some who move from death to life.**

[1] Achtemeier, p204 [2] Eg Exod 22:21–27 [3] Achtemeier, p199, 203

 **BIBLE IN A YEAR:** Isaiah 29,30; Hebrews 1

# PRAYING WITH CONFIDENCE

**Lord, teach me to be real when I pray and to trust you in all circumstances.**

**PSALM 17**

Our first week with Amos has clearly shown that there are right and wrong ways of living. God had stipulated how Israel should act towards the poor, but the people had ignored him. In contrast, the psalmist is aware of God's requirements for covenant faithfulness. His apparently extravagant claims do not imply that he had no sin; rather that his focus was on trying to be the best he could be.[1] In a time of great trouble, the psalmist is misrepresented and surrounded by enemies; if this is David's prayer, then Saul was his physical enemy, but it could easily refer to metaphorical enemies as well.

The psalmist's prayer demonstrates his close relationship with God. He is confident that God will hear him (v 6) and protect him (v 8, instant protection like the automatic blinking of an eye to guard its pupil ['apple'], or like wings covering him, as if God were a mother bird); and that retribution is something that God will do, not the psalmist himself (vs 13,14). He knew that he was held within God's steadfast love (a strong covenant word), that the persecution would end one day 'and that God's presence with him in the future would be as real and as sure as it had been in the past'.[2] There is no developed idea of resurrection in the Old Testament, but perhaps verse 15 gives a hint! Certainly we as Christians can look forward to resurrection with Christ, which is not escapist but a gloriously reassuring reality in hard times.

Wilcock points out that 'the godly life is an effect of God's grace, not of David's exertions. If he pleases God it is only because God has first taken hold of him.'[3] How do you view your own life? Does it demonstrate that God has taken hold of you?

**Which part of this psalm most speaks to you? Allow God to print it on your memory.**

[1] Compare how God speaks of Job (Job 1:8; 42:8) [2] M Wilcock, *The Message of Psalms 1–72*, IVP, 2001, p61 [3] Wilcock, p59

**BIBLE IN A YEAR:** Isaiah 31,32; Psalm 105

# WHAT OF THAT DAY?

**Which is your favourite worship song? Meditate on it now.**

## AMOS 5:18–27

Some lovely friends of mine, a British/German couple, came to live and minister in Britain feeling secure as members of the European Union; at the time of writing, their future looks less secure. In Amos' day, most people who counted for anything would have felt they were enjoying God's favour and that their good life was secure – but it was an ill-placed confidence.

Because of their past experience of God as a warrior, fighting for them, Israel's optimistic belief was that 'the day of the LORD' (v 18) would produce the final destruction of all its enemies. Amos turns the tables and declares that the day Israel is yearning for would result in its own doom and that darkness, gloom and exile lay ahead (vs 18–20). What do we understand by 'the day of the Lord' for us today? Jesus' second coming? Do we desire that? If so, why do we desire it? Will it live up to our expectations, or will we be shocked to realise that we have fallen short of God's requirements of us?

It was in its people's worship that Israel's false idea of the day was perpetuated. Now, in cutting language, God dissociates himself from the people's worship. He cannot stomach the stench or sight of it, when they are abusing it so flagrantly. Scrap the songs and harps (v 23)! How unlike Psalm 33:1–3, where their use is encouraged in true worship! Water is essential for life; verse 24 underlines how vital justice and righteousness are in the believer's lifestyle. We cannot love God if we do not love our neighbours – and not just those we feel comfortable with! 'Concern for the rights and welfare of all his people flows, like a mighty river, from [God's] own heart. Whoever would truly serve him must go with that flow.'[1]

**Take time to reassess your own life and attitudes. Is there any reason why God might reject your worship?**

1 Hubbard, p194

# LIFESTYLE CHALLENGE!

**'All things come from you, and of your own have we given you.'[1] Lord, may I never forget this!**

**AMOS 6**

Whom do the people in your country idolise and try to copy? The celebrities of ancient Israel would have had a lot in common with those of today. Amos' words are addressed to such people in Israel. They were, of course, always rich. They sprawled on the very best furniture; the word 'lie' in verse 4 is used of the spreading tendrils of a wild vine, or loose hanging of fabric.[2] While they lounged, they ate meat (only the rich could afford meat), sang and made music, drank by the bowlful and anointed their bodies with special oils. Their revelry was possibly linked to a social/religious celebration involving inordinate drinking and sacred sexual orgies.[3]

There is nothing wrong with leisure time, good food, enjoyment of music or the use of moisturisers! What was wrong was the attitude of idle self-indulgence, subsidised by the exacting of bribes and levying of taxes on ordinary people. Amos demonstrates the absurdity of deliberate corruption and perversion of justice by likening it to horses running over rocks and oxen ploughing in the sea (v 12). The Israelites were dissolute, taking 'no thought for the fact that their society is rotten to the core, blackened and decaying in its commerce and courts and worship, giving no heed to the covenant demands of a God who is Lord over all.'[4] So the 'foremost nation' (v 1) would be 'among the first to go into exile' (v 7).

We may find it easy to condemn Israel, but how often have we been tempted to excesses ourselves? How much do we spend on new clothes compared with how much we give to charities working among the world's poor? How often do we eat far more than we need – and ignore the world's starving children? Out of sight, out of mind? But God knows.

**Holy Spirit, implant in me a new spirit of self-discipline and generosity.**

1 1 Chr 29:14, NRSV 2 Achtemeier, p217 3 Hubbard, p203 4 Achtemeier, p214

**BIBLE IN A YEAR:** Isaiah 35,36; Hebrews 3

# THREE VISIONS

**'But when I see thee as thou art, I'll praise thee as I ought.'[1] Praise God for his great mercy towards his children.**

## AMOS 7

Amos was a shepherd,[2] a very ordinary person, not trained to the priesthood, yet someone who was passionate about God. He was also *com*passionate and, perhaps because of his agricultural experience, he could empathise with those suffering the devastation of locusts or fire. Hence his moving intercessions for Israel in response to his first two visions (vs 2,5), turning away God's anger (vs 3,6). As Achtemeier points out, God listens to human appeals; nothing is set in concrete. 'The sacred history is really one long dialogue between God and human beings in which there is constant action and reaction.'[3] If you are a church leader, are you ordinary enough to empathise deeply with those in your care? Do you intercede for them with a passion born of a genuine understanding?

There was a third vision, however, and this time there could be no intercession, because measured by God's standards of righteousness and justice, 'the wall of Israel's political and religious life was shown to be tilted beyond repair; it had to come down.'[4] Demolition is always a messy business and the threat of it fanned the priest Amaziah's anger into flame. King Jeroboam I had founded a state religion that was different from that of Israel's covenant past;[5] king and religious system had become inseparable. Notice that Amaziah blamed Amos, not God. There was still incredulity that Amos' prophecies could ever be fulfilled. Amaziah was to discover that Amos was right!

Amos was courageous. He was also completely sure that God had called him to this special task of prophesying to Israel. Is God calling you to a new role in his service? Do you feel too ordinary? Trust him and go with it!

**Lord, may I listen to you and follow your call.**

[1] John Newton, 1725–1807, 'How sweet the Name of Jesus sounds' [2] Amos 1:1
[3] Achtemeier, p220 [4] Hubbard, p215 [5] 1 Kings 12:26–33



**BIBLE IN A YEAR:** Isaiah 37,38; Hebrews 4

# WHAT PRICE GOD'S WORD?

**'Oh, how I love your law! It is my meditation all day long.'[1]**

**AMOS 8**

It's likely that those who read these notes have unlimited access to God's Word in the form of the Bible, and also to preaching, books, perhaps even modern-day prophecy. Is this something we take for granted? What would it be like if all these were taken from us? That is part of what Amos is warning about. There would be a famine of hearing the word of God (vs 11,12).

Amos' fourth vision, a basket of ripe summer fruit, centres on a wordplay in Hebrew. The words for 'summer fruit' and 'end' are very similar. For Amos it is a graphic pointer to how God will make an end of Israel's life as the people know it. With some recapping on earlier themes, Amos declares that the nation is ripe for punishment, because of its unjust and heartless commercial dealings. (Did you notice the hypocrisy of keeping the Sabbath but wanting it to end as soon as possible so the people can continue with their very dubious behaviour?) Their whole way of life will end. Festivals will turn to fasts. Singing to weeping. There was no formal belief in life after death, so the only immortality expected was to live on through one's son.[2] So to weep for the death of an only son was to weep without hope for the future.[3] The end is envisaged in terms of an earthquake and solar eclipse, but the worst thing of all was that there would no longer be any word from God. God would be totally silent. A famine indeed.

Comparison of God's Word to bread is a familiar idea in the Bible.[4] Without food we die. Without God's Word, we die spiritually. It is indispensable and life-giving. Has it become overfamiliar? Do we realise what a huge privilege it is to access it?

**Pray for those who work tirelessly and sometimes in dangerous situations to translate the Bible into indigenous languages.**

1 Ps 119:97, NRSV 2 Cf 1 Sam 24:21 3 Achtemeier, p227
4 Deut 8:3; Isa 55:1–3,10,11; Matt 4:4

# GOD: TERROR OR JOY?

**'If God is for us, who can be against us?'[1] Meditate on what this means to you.**

## AMOS 9:1–10

The bad news continues, but Amos' words evoke memories of other biblical texts, which can help us. The dramatic collapse of the Temple sanctuary begins at the tops of the pillars, going down to the loosened shaky thresholds (v 1). Judgement will be released from top to bottom, showing that it is a divine act like an earthquake, rather than a human assault.[2] It reminds me that when Jesus died to take our own judgement upon himself the curtain of the Temple was torn from top to bottom – an act of God, not of human hand.[3]

Verses 2–4 emphasise that there is nowhere to hide – God's presence will pursue the people wherever they go. Here, it is a horrific picture, but in Psalm 139, the psalmist envisages a different scene, giving us comfort that God's presence accompanies us at all times, in all places.[4] Furthermore, Amos tells the people of Israel that there is nothing that can separate them from God's *wrath*, because trust and obedience are missing, replaced by pride, empty worship, oppression of the helpless and so on. What a relief to read Paul's words to those of us who trust and obey him that nothing in all creation can separate us from God's *love* in Christ Jesus![5]

Verses 5 and 6 are part of an ancient hymn, reinforcing who God is and what he is doing, shaking the nation in the sieve of his judgement (vs 9,10). It is God himself who will bring an end to Israel's life. None will fall through the sieve, because none is good grain.[6] In short, Amos is underlining that 'God's presence is at home everywhere in the universe from top to bottom, and that presence is utterly dependable and permanently to be reckoned with.'[7] This is still true; we take Amos' warnings lightly at our peril.

**Lord, may I never take my salvation for granted, but always love, trust and obey you.**

1 Rom 8:31 2 Eg Hubbard, p242 3 Matt 27:50,51 4 Ps 139:1–12 5 Rom 8:31–39 6 Achtemeier, p232; see tomorrow's note for v 8c 7 Hubbard, p246

 **BIBLE IN A YEAR:** Isaiah 41,42; Hebrews 5

# A HAPPIER ENDING

**Father, thank you that despite the ghastly history of your church at times, you haven't given up on us!**

**AMOS 9:11–15**

The transition from verse 10 to verse 11 has been described as 'abrupt and surprising … The sword of judgement gives way to the trowel of reconstruction.'[1] After all the doom and gloom of the rest of Amos, how can we understand this change? The mention of 'David's fallen shelter' (v 1, implying Jerusalem) hints that Amos' words to the northern kingdom of Israel were relevant also to his own southern nation of Judah, which suffered a similar fate for similar reasons some 135 years after the fall of Israel. Many commentators believe that these last two oracles were written much later, therefore. Others look ahead to a time beyond the judgement. The most compelling thought for me, though, is that Amos never lost sight of the covenant relationship between the Lord and Israel/Judah. God's commitment to his people *had* to lead to the grace of restoration. If judgement is the last word, then human sin has won: God has been unable to attain his goal of salvation for the world and therefore cannot be Lord of heaven and earth. The truth is that he is sovereign and will indeed bring all his good purposes for humanity and his world to fulfilment.[2] The book ends with the words, 'the LORD *your* God' (v 15, italics added) – underlining that personal, loving covenantal relationship.

God can never overlook human sin – but human sin is never the last word. We Christians know that the new David, the Messiah, God's anointed King, has come as the fulfilment of the promise to Abraham.[3] Jesus is the one through whom God will bring blessing and abundant life on all the families of the earth. We know what it cost him to do so. We need to heed the warnings of this book as they apply to us; but we should also never lose sight of the hope of redemption and restoration for those who own him as their Lord and Saviour.

**Father, I stand before you humbled and deeply grateful for your loving perseverance with me, a sinner.**

1 Hubbard, p250 2 Achtemeier, p235 3 Gen 12:1–3; cf Galatians 3:8; Amos 9:11–12 are cited in Acts 15:16–18; see also Achtemeier p236

**BIBLE IN A YEAR:** Isaiah 43,44; Hebrews 6

# LOVE, PRAISE, COMMITMENT

**'The Lord lives! Blessed be my rock, and exalted be the God of my salvation.'[1]**

## PSALM 18

'I love you, Lord' (v 1). When we say that, what do we mean? The word 'love' here is an uncommon Hebrew word which is impulsive and emotional.[2] That definitely has a place in our own experience of profound gratitude to God. Normally in the Bible, to 'love' God is a covenant term implying loyalty and commitment to obedience. It is this underlying theme of covenant righteousness (eg in vs 20–24) that explains David's apparent boastfulness. As in last Sunday's psalm, he is not claiming perfection but is effectively saying, 'I want to walk in your ways, Lord' – a simple prayer that we all need to pray! This psalm is cited in 2 Samuel 22 and belongs to the period described in 2 Samuel 8:13–18, at the zenith of David's career.

In poetic language reminiscent of the Exodus and Sinai,[3] David testifies to what God has done for him at a time of distress and danger and what he trusts he will do in the future. Rescue was part of God's side of the covenant. Hebrew does not have tenses as English does, whence the differences between various translations of (eg) verses 31–45. This allows us to look ahead as well as behind and see the ever-living, active God at work throughout history, into the New Testament and beyond.[4]

David takes up what God has revealed of himself (vs 25,26) and offers it back to him as praise and challenge. 'He makes his creed his prayer.'[5] You are like this, Lord; so do what you've promised: deliver me (v 27), keep my lamp burning (v 28), enable me to cope with people and situations (v 29). This is an excellent foundation for prayer: to start with God's own character. So, the psalm starts and ends in praise! (vs 1–3,46–50).

**Think through some of the reasons that you love God. Tell him about them!**

1 Ps 18:46, NRSV 2 Kidner, p91 3 See Exod 9,10,15,19 4 Wilcock, p68
5 Wilcock, p66

 **BIBLE IN A YEAR:** Isaiah 45,46; Psalm 107

# PHILIPPIANS

## A LETTER FROM PRISON

Imagine you are imprisoned for your faith in Jesus and you are due in court soon (in many parts of the world this is a reality). How would you feel? If you had the opportunity to write a letter, to whom would you write, what would you put in it and what would your prayer requests be? These were the things the apostle Paul had to consider when he was imprisoned in Rome around AD 60 and set out to write a letter to a church he dearly loved - the church in Philippi. Over the next two weeks, you may be surprised by what Paul put in and left out! But first, a bit of context.

According to Acts 16, Philippi was the first city in Europe that Paul visited in response to his so-called 'Macedonian call'. A business woman called Lydia became Paul's first convert, and she offered Paul and Silas the use of her home, as a base from which they could advance the Christian mission in Philippi. Another notable event is Paul's brief time in prison (in Philippi, not Rome) and the conversion of the Roman jailer and his household. His letter to the Philippians reveals that Paul loved this church and would like to visit them again. Nevertheless, he does not shrink from pointing out problems in the church, such as internal divisions, selfish and grumbling attitudes and external threats from Jewish missionaries.

Paul points out that the solution to most issues in the Philippian church can be found in the concept of godly imitation. Besides Christ, who is the obvious model for imitation, Paul also presents himself, his co-worker Timothy, the Philippian church worker Epaphroditus and even mature believers as models for imitation. Each of them imitate Christ in a particular way and so become examples for imitation to others. Instead of merely telling the Philippians what to do, Paul also points them to real-life examples they can observe - and follow.

***Cornelis Bennema***

# A GOOD START

**Lord, I face many challenges and pressures in life, but I choose to give thanks to you for...**

## PHILIPPIANS 1:1–11

First impressions matter. In keeping with the conventions of Graeco-Roman letter writing, Paul starts by mentioning sender, recipient and greetings. No surprises there, but what should get our attention is how Paul introduces himself. In most of his letters, he refers to himself as an apostle of Christ, but in a few – including Philippians – he calls himself a slave of Christ ('servant' is too weak a translation). Why does he do this? Perhaps he wants to identify himself with the slave-status of Christ mentioned in 2:7 ('slave' occurs only in 1:1 and 2:7), showing his readers that he is an imitator of Christ. This would add credibility to his exhortation to the Philippians to imitate Christ.[1] To model what you expect from others is important.

Paul follows his opening with a thanksgiving section (vs 3–11). In Graeco-Roman letters, this would typically be a thanksgiving to the gods for personal benefits received. Paul both adopts and adapts. Accepting the letter-writing model of his day, he fills it with Christian content by giving thanks to the one God he knows personally, not for his benefits but for the Philippian church. Paul knew the world and used its conventions to glorify God and serve his purposes.

In verse 10, we get a glimpse of Paul's intent in ministry – that the Philippian believers may be 'pure and blameless for the day of Christ'. Paul's aim was not simply to preach the gospel or even to plant churches. His goal in ministry was to present 'blameless' churches at the second coming of Christ.[2] Paul is interested in the moral formation of his Christian communities and in this letter he will explain what a Christ-like life looks like.

**Much has changed since Paul's day, but every culture has its customs and conventions. Rather than entirely rejecting or adopting these, we can adapt them meaningfully within a Christian framework.**

[1] Phil 2:4ff [2] 1 Cor 1:8; 2 Cor 1:14; Col 1:22; 1 Thess 3:13

 **BIBLE IN A YEAR:** Isaiah 47,48; Hebrews 7

# THE UNCHAINED GOSPEL

**Lord, I thank you for my circumstances. Please show me how they can advance the gospel.**

**PHILIPPIANS 1:12–18**

With verse 12, Paul moves to the body of the letter. Knowing that his case will come to court soon, Paul shares details of his personal circumstances. He clarifies that he is not imprisoned in Rome for political reasons but for his faith in Christ. He assures his Philippian friends that his imprisonment is working out fine: believers are getting bolder in preaching Christ and the gospel is advancing. For this, Paul is rejoicing. It is important to note that he does not focus on his circumstances but on the advancement of the gospel. He rejoices in prison because he realises that though *he* is in chains, the gospel is not. Adversity can advance the gospel.

Many believers have begun to preach the gospel with more daring and less fear, but unfortunately some have the wrong motives. 'But what does it matter?', Paul exclaims (v 18). Astonishingly, he can look past the misplaced motives of one group of believers and even appreciate that they preach Christ. Paul's gracious attitude, fuelled by his passion for the spread of the gospel, must serve as an example for those of us who tend to focus on our differences - denominational or theological. Proclaiming Christ is everything!

Paul did not use idle words in his correspondence (unlike many users of modern social media), so why did he share this information about his personal circumstances in Rome? Two reasons come to mind. First, because his friends in Philippi were concerned about him, but second, and more crucially, because issues of division were also threatening the church in Philippi.[1] Having the right priorities and perspective on things can help to overcome differences and divisions. Let us keep our eyes on what we have in common (Christ) rather than where we differ.

**Reflect on how your own circumstances might help to advance the gospel. Pray for people who are imprisoned for their faith, that they may gain the insights Paul did.**

[1] Eg Phil 4:2

**BIBLE IN A YEAR:** Isaiah 49,50; Hebrews 8

# NOBLE CHOICES

**'For God so loved the world that he gave his one and only Son.'[1] 'Christ loved us and gave himself up for us.'[2]**

## PHILIPPIANS 1:19–26

Paul ponders his imminent trial and what its outcome might be. A death sentence seems a real possibility, so what are his thoughts about the outcome? If he had a choice – life or death – what would he choose? In verse 21, he sums up the options: (1) 'to live is Christ', where everything in his life is about and for Christ, or (2) 'to die is gain', meaning freedom from earthly troubles and being in Christ's presence.

In verses 21–24, Paul goes back and forth between the two alternatives, but not without reasoning and clarity. In verse 21a, he mentions that to live is Christ and in verse 21b that to die is to be in Christ's presence. In verse 22, to live would mean doing fruitful work; in verse 23, to die would mean being with Christ, which is much better for Paul. In verse 24, for Paul to live is much better for the Philippians. He is torn between the two options but his turmoil ends with him leaning towards what is better for the Philippian church. Having reasoned that the better choice is not what is best for him but for others, Paul knows what the outcome will be: life (v 25).

Again, we must ask why Paul lets us peek into his mind. The answer is that Paul's attitude of choosing what is best for others exemplifies what he will urge the Philippians to do in 2:4, which is to imitate the attitude of Christ. In contrast, the world often tells that we should choose what benefits us. God's biggest choice was to give his Son for us; Jesus' biggest choice was to sacrifice his life for us; Paul's choice was to go on living for the Philippians' sake. All these choices benefited others.

**We make many choices in our lives. Consider how you can be more selfless in your choices: choosing that which will benefit others and the spread of the gospel.**

1 John 3:16 2 Eph 5:2

# MODEL GOSPEL CITIZENS

**'May these words of my mouth and this meditation of my heart be pleasing in your sight, LORD, my Rock and my Redeemer.'[1]**

**PHILIPPIANS 1:27–30**

Having elaborated on his circumstances for the benefit of his Philippian friends, Paul now gives them ethical instructions. Usually, Paul states the central case on which everything depends early on in a letter. Here, he does so in verse 27: 'conduct yourselves in a manner worthy of the gospel of Christ'. The Greek term 'to conduct yourselves' has a political tone, referring to one's life as a citizen.[2] Philippi was a Roman colony and its citizens were proud of their rights and privileges. Hinting at this, Paul urges the Philippian believers to live like proper bearers of the gospel.

In verses 27b and 28a, Paul spells out that such a life includes steadfastness, unity and courage. To 'stand firm in the one Spirit' speaks of a steadfastness or unwavering faithfulness brought about by the Spirit. The imagery in the phrase 'contending as one man' (NIV, 1984) can refer to gladiators fighting side by side in life-or-death situations in the arena, or to soldiers fighting wars in closed ranks. The instruction to the Philippian church not to be divided but to show a united front is a matter of life or death for Paul.[3] If we grasp this, there will be less division, discord and disagreement in some of our churches.

Living a life worthy of the gospel goes together with suffering (v 29). This is because God's society (of which Christians are part) and the world's societies (of which Christians are also part) often have conflicting values and attitudes. For Paul, both faith in Christ and suffering for Christ are privileges granted to the Christian by God. Just as Paul suffered and still suffers for Christ and the gospel, so do the Philippians.

**Christians are both citizens of heaven and citizens of a geopolitical nation. How can you be a model gospel representative in this world, even (or especially) when it creates tension?**

[1] Ps 19:14 [2] RP Martin, *Philippians*, IVP, 1987, p86,87 [3] Martin, *Philippians*, p88,89

# SHARED CHRIST-EXPERIENCES

**'There is one body and one Spirit ... one Lord, one faith, one baptism; one God and Father of all.'[1] Praise God for unity.**

## PHILIPPIANS 2:1–4

Paul now appeals to the shared experience of the Philippians for his moral instructions. The repeated 'If you have any ... if any ... if any' in verse 1 means something like, 'Since you have experienced...'.[2] While some Christians neglect the importance of experience, others tend to overstress it. God has created us as physical beings who experience reality through our senses. These sensory experiences are processed and stored as memories and knowledge, which in turn influence our understanding of the world. Any experience needs interpretation, so our experiences of God must be interpreted in line with biblical truth. For Paul, the believers' shared experience in Christ is the basis for living together in unity and humility.

Having summed up their common experience in Christ, Paul urges the Philippian believers towards unity in verse 2. They should think alike and love alike, being one in mind and purpose. The growth of a church in maturity, purity and effectiveness is in direct proportion to its growth in unity. It appears that the issue of unity in the church was as much an issue in Paul's time as it is today and can only be addressed if we heed Paul's next exhortation.

To strive for unity implies that we let go of 'self'. Paul urges the Philippians to be other-focused: to regard others better than themselves and to see to the interest of others instead of their own. While this seems unachievable, it is the remedy for many of our problems. Most of us take ourselves too seriously and are too busy with our own interests. However, we cannot be Christians by ourselves; we need other Christians so we can grow together through our common experience in Christ. This is difficult and requires an attitude of humility and focus on the 'other'.

**Think how you can contribute to unity in the church. How can you consider others better than yourself and prioritise the interest of others in a practical way?**

1 Eph 4:4–6 2 GF Hawthorne, *Philippians*, Word Books, 1983, p64



**BIBLE IN A YEAR:** Isaiah 55,56; Hebrews 10

# THE EXAMPLE OF CHRIST

**'In bringing many sons and daughters to glory, it was fitting that God ... should make the pioneer of their salvation [Jesus] perfect through what he suffered.'[1]**

**PHILIPPIANS 2:5–11**

Paul now presents the supreme example for imitation. This magnificent 'Christ hymn' probably originated in the early church. It may have been composed for Christological reasons (ie related to the person and work of Christ), but Paul uses it for an ethical purpose, presenting Christ as the ultimate model of moral behaviour. The Christ hymn consists of two parts: humility in the incarnation and crucifixion; and exaltation in the resurrection and ascension.

In verses 3 and 4, Paul urged the Philippian believers humbly to consider the interests of others; here, in verses 6–8, he describes how Christ did precisely that. Unlike Adam, who tried to grasp something that was not his (equality with God), Christ did not take advantage of what was his, but poured himself out (literally 'emptied himself') for the sake of humanity. The idea is not so much of Christ setting aside something but of manifesting the 'form' of God in the 'form' (vs 6,7, NIV notes) of a slave, the lowliest of human beings, in order to serve us, on a cross. Imitating Christ means that every position we hold should become a position of service.

The depth of Christ's humiliation is matched by the height of his cosmic exaltation. Verses 9–11 are not about God making Jesus into something he was not before (he always was the pre-existent, divine Son) but about elevating him to a place of supreme honour and lordship over the universe. The humiliated, crucified Christ is the exalted, cosmic Christ – worthy of worship. Likewise, Christ's becoming a slave was not a temporary status or role but the taking on of a permanent, new identity. Serving others in humility and with their interest at heart is not something to be done occasionally; rather, it should become second nature because we have become servants.

**The world entices us to climb the socio-economic ladder. Instead, are we willing to scale back and follow our downwardly-mobile Lord?**

1 Heb 2:10

# UNIVERSAL AND PARTICULAR

**'The chief end of man is to glorify God and to enjoy him for ever.'[1]
O Lord, may I see both your general and your specific splendour.**

## PSALM 19

The first third of this psalm relates to the universal (vs 1–6) and another third to the particular (vs 7–10) aspects of God's glory. In the universal section, the psalmist delights in God's splendour visible throughout creation. According to a well-known philosophical argument for the existence of God, any design reflects the nature of the designer. So here, the created world continually proclaims the glory of its Creator. In ancient cultures, the sun was often worshipped as a god, but the psalmist asserts that the sun (and everything else) is God's handiwork and exists for his glory. We might want to remind ourselves that only the one true God is worthy of worship and check whether someone or something has taken the place that rightfully belongs to him.

Moving to the section that spells out the particulars, the psalmist expresses delight in God's gift of the Law to the nation of Israel. The Law is not restricted to the Ten Commandments but refers to a way of life in line with God's stipulations for Israel ('Torah' is instruction). In the New Testament, Jesus explains and models the life that God expects from us. Thus, Paul urges Christians to imitate Jesus[2] and to live by the Spirit.[3]

Bringing the universal and the particular together, God created a world where people can live an ordered life and both aspects – the created world and the created order – prompt the psalmist to praise the Creator. The psalmist closes by expressing his desire that his spoken words and unspoken thoughts may be pleasing to God. May our sole desire also be to please God by loving him with our entire heart, soul and might.[4]

**How can you hold together the universal and particular aspects of God's work? How does God's plan for you fit into his overall plan for the world-wide church?**

[1] Westminster Shorter Catechism [2] Phil 2:5–11 [3] Gal 5:16–25 [4] Deut 6:5

 **BIBLE IN A YEAR:** Isaiah 59,60; Psalms 110,111

EWG 183

Scripture Union

Yes! I would like an annual subscription to *Encounter with God* starting with issue OD18.

**THERE ARE 4 WAYS TO ORDER**

***Online:*** www.scriptureunion.org.uk/Encounter • ***By Phone:*** 01908 856 006
Visit your local Christian bookstore • ***By post:*** Return this completed form to
**Freepost SU MAIL ORDER**

Mr / Mrs / Miss / Rev / Other **NAME:**

**ADDRESS:**

**POST CODE:**

**EMAIL:** **TEL:**

*Encounter with God* one year subscriptions starting with OD18 paid by Direct Debit £16 (Saving £1) ☐

*Encounter with God* one year subscriptions starting OD18 £17 ☐

We will use the supplied contact details in relation to your purchase. We'd also really like to let you know about other resources we have to offer. Please select how we can contact you: Email ☐ Post ☐ Phone ☐

Scripture Union will never sell your data or share it with another company or charity for marketing purposes.
View our full privacy policy at scriptureunion.org.uk/privacy

**TO THE RETAILER:** We want your customers reading the Bible regularly. For any queries on subscription prices please contact retailsupport@scriptureunion.org.uk

Scripture Union

Instruction to your Bank or Building Society to pay by Direct Debit

DIRECT Debit

Please fill in the form and send it to: Scripture Union, Trinity House, Opal Court, Opal Drive, Fox Milne, Milton Keynes MK15 0DF
Name and full postal address of your bank or Building Society

To: The Manager Bank/building society

Address

Postcode

Name(s) of Account Holder(s)

Branch Sort Code

Bank/Building Society account number

Service user number

8 4 0 6 5 1

Reference

**Instruction to your Bank or Building Society**
Please pay Scripture Union Direct Debits from the account detailed in this Instruction subject to the safeguards assured by the Direct Debit Guarantee. I understand that this Instruction may remain with Scripture Union and, if so, details will be passed electronically to my Bank/Building Society.

Signature(s)

Date

Banks and Building Societies may not accept Direct Debit Instructions for some types of account.

**SUBSCRIPTION:** £ **GIFT TO SU'S WORK:** £ **I ENCLOSE TOTAL PAYMENT OF:** £ *(IN POUNDS STERLING)* **BY:**

☐ **CHEQUE PAYABLE TO SCRIPTURE UNION** ☐ **POSTAL ORDER** ☐ **PLEASE DEBIT MY CREDIT/DEBIT CARD**

**CARD NO.**

**EXPIRY DATE:** / **ISSUE NO. / VALID FROM:** / **SECURITY NO.**

**DATE:** **CARD HOLDERS SIGNATURE:**